Coming together is a beginning;
keeping together is progress;
working together is success.

Henry Ford

Foreword

Dedicated teachers have always had a vision. Our classrooms were never simply places to work. Our dreams were much bigger. We intuitively discovered ways to nurture and inspire. We looked for ways to build rapport and trust, knowing how much more could be taught in an emotionally healthy environment. We learned from experience that focusing on the affective realm had direct impact on cognitive processing.

Research continues to reinforce the fact that the best teaching merges both thinking and feeling. Neurobiological evidence confirms that what we learn is influenced by our emotions. Studies of learning styles conclude that maximal learning can be orchestrated when the physical sensing and intuition functions of the brain are integrated with thinking and feeling. No longer theory, and far more than just "good ideas that work," this research is translated into useful and practical classroom strategies in *Cooperative Learning and Motivation Across the Curriculum.*

Instilling confidence, building decision-making and problem-solving skills, and structuring the classroom for successful experiences are all within our power. It's part of that vision and certainly part of the promise of teaching. If we are to promote a lifelong love of learning, we need to know the means to initiate excitement and involvement, and we need to create a student workplace which is child-friendly.

"My favorite subject is lunch. I get to sit with my friends and we get to talk. My next favorite subject is recess. I can be with my friends and we can play. I don't have a third favorite subject."

Whoops! Is there something wrong with this picture?

GA1494

If the kindergarten is the only place in your school where tables are set up with chairs around them and students can sit together when they work, perhaps it's time to rethink classroom seating arrangements. The purpose of cooperative learning is to have students working together in groups, a task difficult to accomplish when seated in rows. Communication skills are emphasized in cooperative learning; they are processes hard to practice when looking at the back of someone's head.

Several years ago, Roger Taylor, a well-known researcher and advocate for gifted education, was a workshop speaker at a conference that I attended. Something he said about midway through his presentation has stayed with me. "The most effective teacher," he remarked, "is a guide on the side, not a sage on the stage." Dr. Taylor might well have had cooperative learning in mind, because the "guide on the side" is exactly the role played most of the time in a cooperative learning classroom by the teacher who moves from cooperative group to cooperative group facilitating the learning process.

I have never forgotten that message, and it is probably one that should be printed on a poster and placed in every classroom. Students in lecture-oriented classrooms may be thinking, but the interactive behaviors that occur in cooperative learning classrooms are more productive. Students discuss, observe, compare, imagine, describe, create, listen, evaluate, and problem solve. I believe that all cooperative learning lessons can and should be structured so that students are able to solve a problem, create something, or discover something. There are few lecture situations which can virtually guarantee that one or more of those learning experiences will occur.

Students in cooperative learning groups feel a sense of personal importance, a sense that they belong. This is further enhanced by what researchers are discovering about speaking and listening skills. While students are learning to express themselves clearly and to listen critically through activities which are promoted in cooperative learning groups, researchers note that students' thinking skills are also almost always enhanced.

Small groups in the classroom mirror what children seek outside the classroom—an opportunity to belong and to contribute, and a sense of security. Lunch as a favorite subject? Don't count on it if you institute cooperative learning in your classroom. Maybe lunch will come in third.

GA1494

Cooperative Learning and Motivation
Across the Curriculum

by
Susan Finney

Cover by Kathryn R. Marlin

Copyright © 1994, Good Apple

ISBN No. 0-86653-802-X

Printing No. 987654321

Good Apple
1204 Buchanan St., Box 299
Carthage, IL 62321-0299

Paramount Publishing

Table of Contents

GA1494

How to Use This Book

If the idea behind education is to develop minds that question the world and solve its problems—minds that *use* information instead of just *store* it—the powerful combination of cooperative learning and interdisciplinary instruction has broad implications for motivating students.

A vital strength of cooperative learning is that it encourages new thinking—not "new" in that it has never been discovered, but "new" because it has been produced by the group's participants. Working together, group members construct knowledge. Because this knowledge is new, it is their own. Students are validated as both learners and discoverers as they involve themselves wholly in the subject matter.

Subject matter is also made more relevant to students when cross-curricular connections are purposely incorporated into lesson planning. Where more opportunities are provided for students to make connections between the disciplines, more meaning is created. Curriculum at all levels can merge and then emerge as something new, with instruction which builds understanding and motivation by involving students in their own learning.

The cooperative group is the perfect forum for interdisciplinary instruction. Crossing the disciplines expands perspectives, builds meaning, and increases involvement as the new learnings become mutually reinforcing. Cooperative learning provides opportunities for students to summarize concepts, express ideas, relate to personal experience, verbalize problem solving, voice opinions, and discover relevance in other ways in a supportive group environment.

The strategies and lessons detailed in this book illustrate the diversity of curricular areas which are easily incorporated into interdisciplinary instruction and cooperative learning. The path to reinvigorating a love of learning in your classroom begins here.

The Theory Behind Cooperative Learning (pages 3-6) gives the philosophical background and rationale for fostering a cooperative classroom environment. From my classroom experience and my experience conducting workshops, I recognize that change does not occur easily. So much has been handed to us in the name of instructional improvement that we've become cynical. It helps to understand that the cooperative learning process just didn't suddenly arrive on the scene. It has validity and it has a history, and ongoing research continues to support its great worth.

GA1494

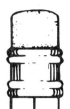

Establishing Cooperative Groups (pages 7 and 8), **The Role of Rules** (page 9), and **The Role of Roles** (page 10) each offer specific, practical suggestions for structuring a cooperative classroom. From deciding how many students should be in each cooperative group to establishing some basic behavioral rules to listing possible roles individual students can hold within their groups, these pages will cover all of the nuts-and-bolts questions that might arise when you begin to restructure your classroom.

Team Building (pages 12 and 13) discusses the importance in and value of promoting a sense of community within cooperative groups. The concept of teamwork and working together towards a common goal should be pervasive. At its best, the bonding and trust which can occur in cooperative group work frequently obviate the need to focus on the rules. But let me offer a caution: it won't happen all at once. It's a process and it needs time to develop. Some **Ideas for Getting Started** are offered on page 14.

The middle sections of this book are devoted to introducing nine different cooperative learning strategies that will help you create an atmosphere of directed, involved, enthusiastic learning in your classroom:

Each strategy is carefully described, and one or more examples are given to illustrate it. Use the examples to help fashion lessons relevant to your specific grade level or subject area. Whether you adapt your own lessons to these cooperative strategies or try out the sample lessons provided, the reproducible **Strategies Grid** (page 16) will serve as a convenient record-keeping device. Use it to jot down the titles of the activities you select or to make notes on how you will be able to integrate the strategies into your lesson plans.

Additional strategies for accessing students' interests, abilities, and creativity are outlined in the last four sections of the book. **Developing a Thinking, Meaning-Centered Curriculum** (pages 64-78), **A Look at Multiple Intelligences** (pages 79 and 80), **Learning Styles** (pages 81-87), and **Brainwaves** (pages 88-91) offer suggestions for adapting the latest discoveries in educational and psychological research to create stimulating, motivating learning experiences within the context of a cooperative classroom structure.

GA1494

The Theory Behind Cooperative Learning

The foundation upon which cooperative learning is based has been "under construction" for several years. Unlike much in education which appears to be the result of that dependable pendulum swing, cooperative learning could not have happened earlier. It has evolved from combinations, amalgamations, and mergers. It is the brainchild of disparate theorists. It is the sum of its many parts.

Great ideas have a way of resurfacing, sometimes added to and enriched in the process. In college courses you probably read more chapters on the psychology and history of education than you wanted to, but integrating that knowledge and finding personal meaning took some years of experience. Many of the great ideas you've read about have never lost their validity. Some have been reworked and renamed, and today's professional magazines often feature articles which hearken back to ideas whose geneses go back to the early years of this century. For that reason, I'd like to briefly highlight some of the major contributors to show how incremental the process has been from which cooperative learning finally emerged. It is fascinating to look back and retrospectively view its conceptual beginnings.

In *Democracy and Education* (1916), John Dewey observed that the classroom should become a genuine community where the emphasis was on social interaction, cooperation, and communication. He believed that the true measure of excellence was the extent to which that sense of community was achieved. Dewey's *Experience and Education* (1938) set stringent criteria for learning experiences. Dewey believed that developmentally appropriate experiences had to enable the individual to create meaning. That idea and his espousal of self-direction are especially relevant to cooperative learning. He was also an early proponent of thematic teaching, before it even had a name, suggesting science be studied in relation to social studies and that reading, writing, and mathematics be taught as learning tools, not as drill.

Thirty years later, Jerome Bruner looked carefully at learner motivation and determined that extending the reflective thinking process to include more active involvement in solution-finding increased initiative, comprehension, and interest in one's own learning. Bruner recommended group discussions for stimulating participation and awareness. All of these factors are important components of the cooperative learning process.

GA1494

Jean Piaget, Hilda Taba, and Benjamin Bloom joined the cadre of foundation builders with their focus on the child and identification of cognitive skills which could be applied to learning virtually anything. The belief that thinking can be taught, that it is an active transaction between the student and information, and that previously learned generalizations and facts can be applied to new situations contributed to the theoretical base behind cooperative learning.

Abraham Maslow and Carl Rogers saw education as a means to self-discovery. Curriculum should bring personal meaning to each learner. A significant addendum to that is cooperative learning's role in building meaning. The relevance of education to interests and society's needs was the focus of Ivan Illich, Michael Scriven, Paulo Freire, and Alvin Toffler. These reconstructionists asked that students be educated to deal with change and social issues and be made more aware of leadership—all of which are concepts recognized as integral to the theory behind cooperative learning. (Recently, however, "relevancy" for its own sake has been downgraded in favor of cultural literacy.)

A brief overview of the beginnings of cooperative learning only partially explains its gradual emergence as a powerful educational tool. What those theorists conjectured and tested, the researchers continued to validate. Communication skills, a sense of community, and positive social interaction are basic to cooperative learning and inherent in an individual's successful school functioning. The qualities of relevancy, personal meaning, and self-direction exemplified in the strategies in this book are the same factors which create lifelong learners.

Effectiveness in all the modalities of language—reading, writing, speaking, listening—is, of necessity, required for entry into the workplace. In cooperative learning classrooms they are practiced with emphasis on active listening and clear expression. Competency in speaking and listening are integral to collaborative work and from a child's earliest years can be strategically and developmentally enhanced. In terms of the dynamics of communication and thinking skill development, the two are interwoven. It is possible in actual classroom practice to *have it all*. What the theorists have generated can be accomplished with cooperative learning.

Education has always responded to trends, perhaps sometimes more readily than it should have. Generally, it is the good ideas that work that are behind those trends that particularly captivate us. It is the coalescing of those ideas which David W. Johnson and Roger T. Johnson recognized as a potential innovation. They successfully inaugurated the cooperative learning movement and are, perhaps, its best-known gurus. Its essence

GA1494

derived from its polyglot foundation, the Johnsons' research-based publications expanded the structure of the movement and prepared the way for others to add on and remodel. They continue to expand and expound as they refine their methodology. With a guide to implementing the Johnsons' approach, Dee Dishon and Pat Wilson O'Leary stressed basic principles and training in cooperative skills. Spencer Kagan, Shlomo Sharan, and Robert Slavin are other names identified with the popularization and promulgation of cooperative group learning.

As eclectic as their varied approaches may be, all of these theorists are essentially in agreement regarding some of the fundamental elements of cooperative learning: face-to-face interaction in learning groups, a sense of positive interdependence among group members (Johnson and Johnson call this the "sink or swim together" approach), individual accountability for each group member, and the teaching of collaborative skills for working together effectively.

The major limitation for the classroom teacher, which in no way detracts from the quality of the theory, the credibility of the authors, or the excellence of the materials, is that of ease of integrating theory into classroom practice. At every workshop on cooperative learning that I've conducted, the concerns are focused on adaptation of strategies to existing curricula. Plans for individual and group accountability, structuring positive interdependence, and monitoring the development of social skills are all important but for practical purposes somewhat obscure the issue in which the classroom teacher is most interested–what are the strategies I can use, and how can I adapt my lessons to them?

This book will help answer those questions. With strategies clearly described and further illustrated with sample lessons, the theoretical issues are interwoven with the curriculum presented. Content is integrated with communication experiences. The cooperative group as both audience and individual builds understandings together. Learning experiences are offered which provide for intrigue and build cognitive awareness. Piaget's dual elements of cognition, assimilation, and accommodation are present in full force. The interaction in cooperative groups allows for discovery, awareness, rediscovery, and increased perception as new information is actively processed. As the new ideas interact with the old, rearranging and realigning occur as children in cooperative groups create meaning for themselves.

5

GA1494

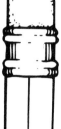

What else happens in cooperative groups? Nurture happens. Self-confidence, responsibility, growth of organizational skills, decision-making, experimenting, exploring, learning from others, experiencing feelings, reflecting, discussing, empathizing, and motivation happen. You will start hearing the words *we* and *our* instead of *I* and *my*. You will have time to guide students in the development of interpersonal skills and concurrently see their feelings of self-worth increase as they become more competent. As they acquire new information, skills, and abilities and can express themselves and listen to others, they begin to realize that human beings are alike in many ways—and unique within those commonalities.

As an astute teacher, you can capitalize on cooperative learning to develop critical thinking and problem-solving skills. And, as you choose among the strategies presented, you can perpetuate the "student as worker" focus. For your students to consciously recognize that the classroom is their workplace and that a workplace can be exciting is of indisputable worth. The revelation that subject matter can be interesting is of incalculable value.

The next move is yours. I encourage you to begin integrating these strategies into your lessons as soon as possible. Begin with something familiar and adapt it to one of the strategies that most appeals to you. Try several different lessons in different curricular areas using the same strategy. Allow your students the latitude to adjust to the group structure. You will discover that the transition will be exhilarating and that soon you won't remember that you taught a particular lesson in any other way. The strategies you feel most comfortable with will soon feel natural to you, and your students will respond similarly.

Each of the strategies is thoroughly discussed, and examples across the curriculum follow in such a way as to make it almost a recipe and as useful as possible. This guide offers strategies which teach subject matter in an unpressured format, strategies planned for stimulation and enjoyment, and strategies engineered so that children can learn how to learn and develop positive attitudes toward their own education. The strategies not only teach subject matter, but subject matter becomes the means by which students are taught how to learn!

It is in those classrooms where cooperative learning plays a major role in a teacher's repertoire that children can become motivated, active learners and those promises can be kept. Let it be your classroom!

GA1494

Establishing Cooperative Groups

Groups of four, which are structured heterogeneously, are accepted as the traditional cooperative learning model. While there may be times when you will group students in other ways, both research and experience have confirmed the desirability of that configuration. It conveys a sense of connectedness needed by children for the interaction which is to occur. Desks and tables should be arranged so that each group of four is seated together and is somewhat separated from the other groups. If that isn't workable, attempt to create a seating arrangement which can be easily rearranged to accommodate a change to groups of four for cooperative activities. In settings where the numbers won't allow for groups of four, three or five will work; but groups of four are most desirable because each group member then has someone with whom to communicate.

Deciding who is to be in each group can be as arbitrary or as planned as your particular teaching style dictates. Knowing your students, you may wish to group two of high ability, one of average ability, and one of lower ability. You may wish to take cards with your students' names on them, shuffle them, and arbitrarily distribute them in groups of four. Some cooperative learning practitioners have used a deck of cards turned so that their numbers can't be seen. Each student draws a card, and then all of the twos sit together, etc. This may be done with the students present or before they enter the room. To avoid potentially negative situations there are advantages to explaining how you will establish groups, if you are doing it arbitrarily, and then setting them up prior to the arrival of students.

Some authors suggest that children simply be seated together for two or three weeks before any formal cooperative strategies are introduced. During that time groups would work together with no particular structure, except that they would begin to see themselves as groups. Everyday tasks might be assigned to different groups to begin fostering interaction and cooperative behaviors. Contrarily, it has also been recommended that the strategies be implemented at the same time groups are established. Interestingly, it works both ways. Much is dependent on the makeup of your particular group of children as well as your willingness and enthusiasm. Any time change is introduced, there will be some resistance. Once your students have experienced cooperative learning, the excitement and involvement intrinsic to it are your best argument for this innovation.

GA1494

One question that is always asked refers to the length of time groups should stay together. There should be adequate time for bonding to occur and projects to be completed. Six to eight weeks has always seemed ideal, but again there are varying viewpoints. One of the advantages of cooperative learning is that, as a process, it is still "becoming." It is flexible and adaptable and little is carved in stone.

Relationships among group members may be nurtured not only by patience, but by the purposeful choices of activities. While the strategies themselves create opportunities for interdependence, you will discover that the ways children view themselves in a group context are primarily reflections of their self-esteem. Changes in one's view of oneself can occur over time. This self-discovery is accelerated through the group's interactions. How children feel relating to others has definite implications for the successful functioning of the group. Maslow has said that respect and approval from others, actual achievement, and learning to accept oneself are the three major factors that influence self-esteem. The cooperative setting can positively act upon all three.

In a heterogeneous cooperative group, individual differences can be effectively accommodated as special abilities are recognized and encouraged. A variety of responses are allowed, improvisation within the group occurs, everybody is listened to, and every group member has recognized standing. The collaborative and interactive learning opportunities in this book are designed to cope with student diversity, build appreciation for differences, and promote an emotionally healthy social environment in which learning from and about others serves also to validate one's self.

8

GA1494

The Role of Rules

In an ideal world, classroom rules would be unnecessary and behavior would always be appropriate. However, whether they are posted on the wall or understood and unspoken, rules are an extremely important part of a well-managed classroom. Rules are a necessity as you begin to use cooperative learning strategies. They serve to reinforce your own management system and clarify appropriate behaviors for group members. As teamwork develops, less emphasis is necessary, but the effectiveness of group interaction and the developing interdependence among group members are greatly enhanced when the following rules are routinely discussed and enforced.

- Every person in your group gets equal time to be heard.
- Every person in your group is responsible for his or her own behavior.
- Every person in your group must be willing to help any group member who asks for assistance.
- If there are questions, check with every person in your group before asking the teacher.

These rules facilitate the development of the cooperative group as a support system. Working in tandem with the various strategies, the rules promote a greater likelihood of enhancing individual competency as well as group proficiency. As you gain insight into the purposeful structure of the cooperative group, you will also recognize that the skills associated with cooperative learning include the development of empathy for others. For many children, that will be a unique experience. It is not often that we can structure practice in caring and sharing as we improve classroom learning. Since group members bring diverse past experiences to the group, the rules also provide a basis for cultivating a common commitment.

To increase the likelihood of success for all the cooperative strategies, it is a good idea to go over the rules frequently in the beginning. Their positive phrasing provides a model so that they may be remembered in positive terms. It doesn't take long for students to remember the rules, but the enthusiasm which cooperative learning engenders does make for noisier classrooms and reinforces the need to set your own behavioral parameters.

Remember, however, that thinking and talking about thinking engage students both emotionally and intellectually and are the basis of effective collaborative work. Inextricably interwoven are the modalities of language–thinking, listening, and communicating. Using arranged environments with carefully structured strategies and rules, teachers can guide interactions to help children acquire a multitude of skills.

GA1494

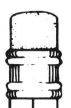

The Role of Roles

Entire chapters have been written regarding the assigning of roles within cooperative groups. Lengthy discussions have focused on the principles of distributed leadership to ensure that all students learn to contribute as active participants. The literature abounds with labels created for all four group members so that each not only feels useful, but is actively involved.

In my classroom experience, I have discovered that the concern for the labels and the attempt to understand what the roles consist of are so consuming as to undermine the process. What is important to realize is that if the cooperative strategy is well designed, positions do not need to be contrived in order to involve students. When role assignments are made, they should be on a temporary basis, so that a responsibility does not become onerous or artificial. In classrooms where cooperative skills are emerging and students are becoming more involved in their own learning, cooperative group roles will be fluid and everchanging. For many lessons which you will teach in a cooperative format, there need be no roles specifically defined.

Suggestions are occasionally made in this book for providing those roles that are seen as necessary, or those which add interest to a specific strategy or lesson. You should, however, feel free to adapt roles on an as-needed basis to fit your group and your teaching style.

The roles most often mentioned in the literature include the following: reader, recorder or scribe, reporter, observer, encourager, questioner, doer, prober, summarizer, checker, praiser, facilitator, caretaker, timer, and monitor. Job descriptions for each of these roles can be found on page 11.

One of the most equitable ways to assign roles is on a rotating basis. When a job is required by one of the activities, suggest that the children number themselves one through four and that jobs be assigned by number. Using a check-off sheet, you can be sure that each group member has varied role responsibilities. Assign tasks by number, saying "All the number threes are readers for this activity." In another instance: "If you are a number four, you are a recorder." In this way, there is accountability, and the jobs that are assigned are relevant and meaningful.

It is easy to get bogged down if you worry too much about the names of the roles or concern yourself with each student having a formal role each time you use a cooperative learning strategy. Get into the cooperative process; try converting some everyday classroom procedures into a cooperative format (for example, cooperative groups taking responsibility for attendance, current events reporting, activity planning), so that your students become comfortable with the behaviors. Use the list of "Positions Available" to create valid relationships, not manufactured ones, among group members by assigning roles only to promote group effectiveness.

Positions Available

The **READER** assumes responsibility for reading any required information to the group.

The **RECORDER** or **SCRIBE** may do the writing for the group when a group product is required.

The **REPORTER** is designated as the group member who will report the group's conclusions to the entire class.

The **OBSERVER** evaluates group effectiveness by sitting outside of the group and commenting during a debriefing.

The **ENCOURAGER** invites reluctant participants to become more active.

The **QUESTIONER** may take responsibility for leading the group by asking questions which are part of an activity or may be the one designated to ask the teacher a group question.

The **DOER** may divide a task into its component parts and assign different jobs.

The **PROBER** looks inquiringly at the possibilities. (Hopefully, this will be most children.)

The **SUMMARIZER** may review directions and also conclusions.

The **CHECKER** makes sure that each group member knows the correct responses and understands the information.

The **PRAISER** offers positive comments.

The **FACILITATOR** ensures that everyone in the group is involved and contributes.

The **CARETAKER** keeps a folder of work and assignments for any member of the cooperative group who may be absent. (This is one position which should be ongoing, although held on a rotating basis.)

The **TIMER** keeps an eye on the clock for those assignments with time limits.

The **MONITOR** keeps the group on task.

GA1494

Team Building

The feeling of camaraderie which pervades successful athletic teams is also necessary to the success of cooperative learning groups. Having said that, however, it is important to note that team spirit evolves as teams perform, and its evolution is the result of the experiences the team has together. In the classroom, as on a playing field, it is practice, practice, practice which bonds students into effective teams.

Fortunately, there are a variety of activities which easily translate into practice sessions. Many of these activities are like those used to stimulate creative thinking. Typical of these tasks are those that ask students to think of unusual uses for objects or to make lists. A sampling of those activities is listed on page 14. Their purpose is to initiate team spirit. If your students have never been grouped heterogeneously and have had few experiences working cooperatively toward a common goal, these programmed activities introduce positive interdependence experientially. These activities are equally valuable in classrooms in which students know one another quite well and in situations where students are meeting for the first time. However, when a team is initially formed, the strangeness can be alleviated by involving them in some common effort as soon as possible.

As you embark on this journey, remember that there are a number of commercial materials available (board games, puzzles, and word games) which can easily be adapted for the purpose of reinforcing esprit de corps and bonding. In addition, group solutions to crossword puzzles, logic problems, and analogies are other effective ways of promoting bonding. Creating a poem using group members' names or a poster naming the group is one more bonding activity. A collage created to symbolize the group serves the same purpose and is also an effective initial team building activity.

Since the purpose of cooperative learning is to effectively incorporate the teaching of content material, the skills of communication and the reality of problem solving through teamwork, it is important that these practice activities be used for readiness, reinforcement, or sponge activities (short, meaningful learning exercises designed to fill time gaps or transition periods) and not remain the sole experience you have with cooperative learning.

GA1494

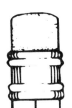

Once team building begins and you regularly integrate cooperative learning strategies into your classroom, the collaborative work itself reinforces team bonding. Meaningful academic work, focusing on group solution-finding, will generate true collaboration.

To move into the reality of cooperative learning, choose a strategy such as "Teams as Teachers" and use it during the day for reviewing simple facts related to a social studies unit. Use the same strategy on the following day as groups work collaboratively to solve logic problems. On a consecutive day, use the identical strategy in language arts for identifying parts of speech. Each time a strategy is used, try it in a different curricular area. The strategies can be moved through the subject areas as you build in opportunities to help your students practice collaborative work. It must be reiterated that the cooperative activities which involve subject matter learning are themselves team building, so move into them as quickly as you can.

GA1494

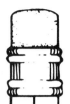

Ideas for Getting Started

The following ideas are simple ways of getting students to work together as a team. Many are paper-and-pencil activities. Pass one pencil and one sheet of paper around to group members eliciting one response at a time from each person. Only one or two of the following ideas should be used at a time, and allotting only five to ten minutes for most of them will keep interest high. You should remain in control of the time parameters so that the game itself does not overshadow the team-building purpose.

The sense of ownership which each cooperative group feels toward its collective effort is an integral factor in team building. To capitalize on that sense of group ownership, time should be allowed to share "favorite" group responses. A representative from each group might choose three or four of the group's most original responses to share with the entire class.

The following suggestions are just a few of the possibilities:
- Make a list of all the things you can think of that make noise.
- Write as many compound words as you can think of.
- Write a sentence for each letter of the alphabet where all words begin with that letter.
- Make a list of things you hate to do.
- Make a list of your favorite things to do.
- Brainstorm uses for a muffin tin.
- Name twenty things which are round and can be thrown long distances.
- Think of unusual uses for a bucket.
- List objects which are red.
- Name ice-cream flavors.
- Invent ice-cream flavors.
- What would you be unable to do if you couldn't read?
- Generate new school rules.
- List situations when a smile is a good idea.
- List situations when a smile is not a good idea.
- When have you been at the right place at the right time?
- How many uses can you think of for a paper plate?
- If you had wings, what could you do that you can't do now?
- List reasons for not going to school.
- List reasons for going to school.
- How would life be different if there were no clocks?
- List dog breeds, cars, flowers, movie titles, cartoon characters, etc.

14

GA1494

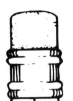

Team Building with a "Twist"

The sense of teamwork that characterizes successful cooperative group work can be achieved only with practice. Groups must be given frequent opportunities to pursue a common goal–a goal which is, most often, a classroom assignment. Team spirit evolves as teams perform, and the experiences which can be orchestrated by the teacher are the key to productive groups.

There are many activities which, traditionally, have been done independently by students; many of these transfer to a cooperative setting and produce far more than a completed work sheet. The collaborative work reinforces team bonding, with group solution-finding generating true collaboration. These activities introduce positive interdependence by giving students experience with it. There are many examples on the following pages.

Combining interdependence with the teaching of content material is, of course, a major focus of cooperative learning. The activities suggested on the following pages will either introduce or reinforce previous classroom learnings, and add a new "twist" to both skill-building and the adventure of bringing humor into the classroom.

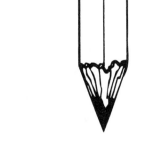

GA1494

Cooperative Learning Strategies Grid

Strategies	Lesson	Lesson	Lesson
Highlighting			
Lend-a-Hand			
Perspective			
Round and Round			
Merry-Go-Round			
Short Circuit			
Testwise			
Teams as Teachers			
Co-op Connections			

GA1494

Cooperative Questioning

Why do we spend so much time in our classrooms asking questions? The most obvious reason is to determine whether our students have learned what we have set out to teach. We also question to prompt more in-depth thinking and, collaterally, more in-depth learning. Effective classroom questioning techniques have always been a concern of educators and have also been the focus of ongoing research. The results of that research have great impact for educators.

Some of the research has confirmed what we already know–there are specific types of questions which are a better fit for some areas of the curriculum than others. What may be relatively new information is that questioning techniques can be accommodated to specific learning styles. That is, some students will respond to a particular type of question better than they would to another. Think about the kind of questions you prefer to be asked when you are in a test-taking situation–are you a multiple choice person or a true-false person? Do you prefer essay questions which allow you to express your opinions or do you enjoy comparing and contrasting? Researchers have identified the types of questions preferred by different types of learners. The implications are definitely far-reaching.

A teacher familiar with a variety of questioning techniques can better meet the needs of all students. The cooperative learning strategies introduced in this book incorporate an abundance of those questioning techniques, the practice of which is most effectively demonstrated in collaborative group work. The reason collaborative group work is such a powerful forum for differing questioning strategies is that within each group are four individuals whose strengths differ. The collaborative effort required by careful question design, where differing strengths are considered, will involve each individual.

Because in many traditional classrooms it is possible for a large percentage of our students to come to school and never be called on, and since questioning in classroom-sized groups usually means that one student is answering and thirty or so students are playing a passive role, for whatever reason, our responsibility is to create an environment where "business as usual" isn't.

What this means is that no matter how much we know about teacher behaviors, cognitive research related to learning styles, multiple intelligences, and brain function, what has to be brought into classrooms is a way to provide opportunities for more children to be able to give answers to our questions. One way to do that is to structure the classroom so that students are in cooperative groups. The cooperative group gives one student at a time in a group of four many more opportunities to contribute

GA1494

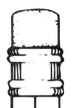

than a class-sized grouping does. Combining increased opportunities for individual students to respond within groups and the additional information about questioning and student learning styles, the bottom line can't be anything but improved teaching.

Because the skills of effective speaking and thinking can be influenced by questioning techniques, our focus here is to create a classroom environment in which all children are involved in the critical and creative thinking needed for producing quality responses. A great deal has been written about levels of questioning, affective involvement, and presenting content that addresses types of intelligence. Texts and teachers' manuals frequently provide visual aids for us in the margin next to the end-of-the-chapter questions: analysis, synthesis, knowledge/recall, etc., to remind us to be ever vigilant. The reason this section has been written, however, is easily as important—what are we doing to provide opportunites for children to give answers?

In the cooperative group setting, specifically in a group of four, questions directed to the entire class can be discussed by a few students in a number of different formats. Thus, all kinds of questions, including those much-maligned "lower-level questions," have value. The value lies in having a chance to respond, to practice listening and speaking skills, to think out loud, to problem-solve, and to produce knowledge.

The following pages detail specific questioning techniques and suggest some appropriate cooperative strategies to use with them. Illustrative lessons are also provided, and lessons throughout these books reinforce the ideas outlined here. Questioning techniques which address varying learning styles and subject matter needs can be used in every area of the curriculum. If your goal is to involve all students in the questioning process, to nurture thinking skill development as well as oral language skills, it makes sense to give your students lots of practice, and this is the way to do it.

The chart on the following page refers to the cooperative learning strategies introduced in this book. The strategies are listed in the first column, while in the second column the questioning techniques most effectively used with that strategy are named. The third column is intended for your use as a visual organizer and planner. Write in it the lessons which you have used or plan to use with a particular strategy, taking into consideration the type of questioning your lesson requires. While there are no hard and fast rules about strategies and questioning, some strategies simply work better than others for particular types of lessons. You will also notice that many questioning techniques are useful in more than one strategy. As you experiment, you'll discover which ones work best for your purposes.

GA1494

Cooperative Learning Strategy	Questions That Ask the Student to . . .	Lessons
1. Highlighting	Choose Interpret Categorize Analyze	
2. Lend-a-Hand	Recall facts Generate ideas Summarize Categorize Follow directions	
3. Perspective	Empathize Compare and contrast Imagine Think metaphorically Evaluate	
4. Round and Round	Generate ideas Imagine Describe feelings Summarize	
5. Merry-Go-Round	Generate ideas Discuss advantages and disadvantages Evaluate Describe feelings Ask questions	
6. Short Circuit	Describe feelings Empathize Create questions Imagine Observe	
7. Testwise	Recall facts Categorize Summarize Hypothesize Create questions Follow directions	
8. Teams as Teachers	Be literal Recall facts Remember details Create questions Follow directions	
9. Co-op Connections	Hypothesize Determine cause and effect Search for patterns Generate ideas	

GA1494

Highlighting

Highlighting is a strategy that capitalizes on the novelty of using highlighting markers and provides teachers with a lesson-specific format which keeps children's interest alive. There is a certain "power" which children feel when they are allowed, even instructed, to mark text, so each student will need both a highlighting pen and a copy of the selection to be studied. What they will be marking will be up to you, depending on what the objective of the lesson is.

Highlighting pens are a wonderful invention when used for the purpose of studying, and they can also be used productively as a teaching tool. Highlighting encourages children to pay close attention to the written word and challenges them to make decisions which have relevance to lesson objectives. The sharing of thoughts which is a direct by-product of this strategy gives children the occasion to listen and be listened to.

One way to use the markers is to ask students to highlight phrases in a story that are especially descriptive, or to find lines in a poem that appeal to them, or words in an essay that detail action. To teach literary devices–metaphors, similes, personification, imagery, alliteration, onomatopoeia, etc.–ask the children to find and highlight all the examples they can.

This becomes a cooperative lesson after enough time has been allotted for the initial search. Children in cooperative groups may share, in structured numerical order, the reasons for their choices. Through discussion, what was abstract becomes concrete. With slight variations, this technique can be applied across the curriculum. As the children work through the document you've chosen and discuss their choices within their cooperative groups, the individual and collective involvement brings meaning to the experience.

This process begins individually, becomes collaborative, and finally may involve a whole class discussion. If curriculum integration is part of your objective, each step of the process lends itself to increased awareness. Asking the question "What did you learn when you worked together?" reinforces new learning and the awareness that four heads may be better than one. The ability to generalize new information and its subsequent transfer are added student benefits of Highlighting.

GA1494

The Story of Rostevan, King of Arabs

Any Highlighting activity has the added advantage of a little magic–a simple highlighting pen. That pen and the literature you select are integral to the effectiveness of this strategy. Whatever literature is chosen, it must be age-appropriate. The poem on page 22 is an excerpt from a book-length saga. It might be used with sixth grade students, but it is probably most appropriate for junior high and/or high school age students. The imagery is sophisticated and allows for a variety of assignments, but it is important to remember that there is a fine line between overanalyzing and developing appreciation.

Another point which has been made before and must be reiterated here is that poetry should not be presented in a vacuum. This particular poem would be wonderfully relevant as part of an interdisciplinary study of the history of the former Soviet Union. For our purposes, it provides an excellent example of integrating literature and history–one of the easiest and most effective curricular combinations to be made.

Explain to your students that Rostevan was a king, and that the poet Rustaveli used a great many adjectives to describe him. You may wish to read this powerful poem aloud, emphasizing those words. Ask students to use their highlighters to mark as many adjectives as they can find which portray the king. (Tell them to concentrate on the first and third stanzas and to use their dictionaries to check parts of speech.)

Next, students in their cooperative groups may compare the words that have been highlighted, marking any that have been missed. (If mistakes have been made, there are no grades given and a clean copy of the poem can be provided later.) There are many beautiful phrases incorporating personification, metaphors, and similes; ask your pupils to find and highlight three or four which they particularly liked.

The group interaction occurs after the highlighting does. In numerical order, your students should share within their groups the reasons for their choices. The meaning behind the phrases can be discussed; conjecture and inferences are encouraged. Greater clarification may occur at a later time during whole-group discussion, or each group can be assigned a stanza to "translate" and explain to the entire group.

Sharing, but not imposing, your impressions of the beauty of the language used reinforces the development of appreciation and builds rapport as well.

GA1494

Shota Rustaveli lived in the Soviet republic of Georgia hundreds of years ago. This is part of a poem called "The Knight in the Panther's Skin" which he wrote to tell the story of the Arabs who conquered Georgia in the seventh century. Rustaveli lived in the twelfth century and was in love with Queen Tamar, who ruled Georgia during that time.

The Story of Rostevan, King of Arabs

Rostevan ruled in Arabia, a monarch exalted and mighty,
Fortunate, noble, farseeing, wise in council and judgement;
The hosts he commanded were countless, he, the invincible warrior;
His speech was fluent and gracious, his bounty and wisdom boundless.

He had one fair daughter, bright as the sun in its glory,
Shedding radiant beams, ravishing all who beheld her.
Hearts and minds were enslaved, all bowed down to her beauty.
Even the sage and the poet were deprived of speech in her presence.

Tinatin, fairest of maidens, grew to be fairest of women;
The sun itself in the sky paled above her in envy.
Rostevan summoned his viziers, graciously ranged them before him;
Proud, majestic, yet mild, he wanted their judgment and counsel.

"We are assembled," he said, "to discuss and counsel together.
The sun of my days is set, a moonless night is before me.
The full-blown rose must scatter the face of the earth with its petals.
But the bud on the branch unfolds, filling the garden with fragrance."

"Mine is the burden of age, sorest affliction of mortals;
The footsteps of death draw near me and I must yield up my spirit.
Light can no longer exist when the shadow of night overtakes it.
Take for your sovereign, my daughter, whom even the sun cannot rival."

The viziers answered: "O King! Speak not of age and of darkness!
One bad counsel from you is better than a hundred good counsels from others.
You have done well to unload your heart of its onerous burden;
She who outshines the sun we name our monarch and ruler.

"Woman she is, but a woman born to rule over a kingdom.
Truly our hearts declare her worthy to be our sovereign.
Her noble deeds, like her radiance, shed brightness and warmth like sunshine.
The lion's whelp is a lion, be it male or female."

22

GA1494

Idiomatic Expressions

The following story (pages 24 and 25) about Jacques-Yves Cousteau is another sample activity designed to spark ideas for using Highlighting in your classroom. It incorporates twelve idiomatic expressions. Students trying to make sense of their literal meanings will have little luck. A suggestion might be to instruct your students to read the story and use their highlighting pens to mark phrases they don't understand. (This strategy may be used in other instances to mark new vocabulary words, adjectives, verbs or other parts of speech, and possibly, examples of humor. The uses of Highlighting are limited only by the imagination.)

The idioms below are included in E.D. Hirsch, Jr.'s *Dictionary of Cultural Literacy*. To maximize involvement in a project of this sort, students may be instructed to solicit the help of their parents for definitions, to guess, or to try the dictionary. Each identified phrase should be written down and numbered along with its definition for accountability. Collaborative group work following independent work is also suggested. As a follow-up, an assignment which requires that a story be written incorporating several of the idioms could be a group-generated project.

1. **hit the ceiling**–to become extremely angry
2. **till the cows come home**–for a long time
3. **hook, line, and sinker**–completely and without reservation
4. **face the music**–to accept unpleasant consequences
5. **bite the bullet**–to adjust to unpleasant circumstances
6. **cool one's heels**–wait for a long time
7. **cry over spilt milk**–to dwell on past misfortunes
8. **sour grapes**–refers to things people decide are not worth having only after they find they cannot have them
9. **wet behind the ears**–inexperienced
10. **feather in his cap**–an accomplishment to be proud of
11. **nose to the grindstone**–to work extremely hard
12. **make no bones about it**–to be blunt and candid about something

Jacques-Yves Cousteau

Jacques' mother hit the ceiling. "Where are we going to put *this* invention?" she asked him. "The room will probably be a mess till the cows come home!" Jacques had just created a working model of a crane and was already at work on a three-foot-long, battery-powered car. "This one goes in the garage," she said. "There's no more room in the house!"

Jacques smiled. His mother wasn't really mad, but it might be a good time to go for a walk along the beach. He watched the waves slowly form and move toward him on the shore. He had learned to swim just recently and he decided to go for a swim. He loved the ocean hook, line, and sinker.

When he returned home, his parents were looking very seriously at him. They had heard he'd been misbehaving at school. It was time to face the music. "We think it is time for you to make some decisions," his father said. "You will never get into the Naval Academy if you do not study harder."

"You must think about those dreams of yours," his mother added. "If you want to make those dreams real, you will have to take responsibility for them."

His parents' words made Jacques think. He did have dreams. He had many ideas of how his life was to be. He would go into the Naval Academy, then the French Navy, and then he would become a pilot. He decided it was time to bite the bullet and prepare himself to pass the test to get into the French Naval Academy.

He did get into the Naval Academy; but just before he was to receive his pilot's wings, an automobile accident created a major interruption in his life. Two broken arms meant he had to cool his heels. To help him regain strength in his arms, his friends suggested that he take up swimming. He remembered how much he loved the ocean and decided he couldn't cry over spilt milk any longer.

One day, a friend brought him a gift which was to change his life. "Those are the goggles that the pearl divers in the South Seas wear so they can find the oysters underwater, Jacques. Maybe you'll enjoy wearing them while you're swimming."

Jacques was out the door. The history of underwater swimming and diving began just at that moment! He didn't know that he was beginning a new era of underwater exploration; he just knew how excited he was about seeing so well underwater. He was caught up in the ideas he had. The ocean was to become his laboratory as his imagination helped him develop more and more ideas.

GA1494

Jacques dreamed of being able to swim underwater like a fish without having to wear a deep-sea diving suit, which was at that time the only way to stay underwater for a long period. He designed a face mask and a tank which could be strapped to his back. Deep-sea divers looked at his invention and told him it would never work, that he looked like a strange kind of fish. Jacques decided it was just sour grapes.

"It may look kind of funny," he said, "but I'm not wet behind the ears. With this aqualung I don't need an air hose from a ship." Jacques-Yves Cousteau had not become a pilot, but he had become an explorer, an inventor, and a discoverer. He learned that if you use your imagination, there was an ocean full of possibilities.

The aqualung and underwater photographic equipment were the beginning. They were feathers in his cap. His imagination created those inventions, but it was keeping his nose to the grindstone that made them a reality. He named his research ship *Calypso*, and it was there that specially designed camera equipment took the first underwater color films for television.

He went on to develop a small submarine. He knew that a diving saucer carrying two men could go deeper than a man could and that it could be used when men lived beneath the sea. He made no bones about it. Jacques believed that men could live in undersea villages created with bubbles made of steel, and he made it happen.

So, perhaps the next time you watch one of the Jacques-Yves Cousteau television specials, you'll remember this story about a small boy whose mother wondered where she'd find room to put his latest invention. And you'll remember, too, that he made his dreams become real.

GA1494

Lend-a-Hand

The main premise of **Lend-a-Hand** is that work is divided so that each group member has specific duties to accomplish that are part of a larger whole. This could be finding the answers to part of a list of questions or the definitions to part of a list of vocabulary words, doing research on part of a report, or taking responsibility for some part of a project. It then becomes the charge of each individual within the cooperative group to teach the other members of the group what he or she knows. It is the obligation of the teacher/facilitator to provide instruction or model the methods which are most effective for doing that.

This strategy is quite similar to the Jigsaw approach sometimes described in other publications on cooperative learning. It is a simplified version, however, which requires little if any preparation. I have found that any strategy which requires a great deal of pre-planning or major revision in lesson format is simply not going to be used by most teachers. They are just too busy. Because Lend-a-Hand works beautifully in a myriad of situations, the key is to use it only if it fits, and you'll find that it fits in many places and serves many purposes.

Grade level appropriateness is particularly important with Lend-a-Hand. It can easily be used in the intermediate elementary grades (4, 5, and 6) and certainly at middle school and above. It must be remembered that children should be able to assume responsibility and be ready to be accountable before it is attempted. Cooperative group members become peer tutors as well as a support system.

One added advantage that you will particularly enjoy with this strategy is that it helps students begin to take control of their own learning. It is one of the many ways discussed in this book that puts you, in Roger Taylor's terms, in the position of a "guide on the side" rather than a "sage on the stage." Moving away from the lectern or podium and away from the position of perennial lecturer, Lend-a-Hand helps to turn your classroom into a "laboratory for learning." You are the facilitator of learning; your students, the workers.

GA1494

Combining Themes in Literature and Poetry

For every age and grade level there are subject matter areas which are prerequisites, regardless of the area of the country in which one resides. Dinosaurs, reptiles, whales, Egypt, seasons, state histories, the universe, the community, holidays, and American history are but a few of these "universals." In whole language and thematically integrated classrooms, clever teachers have added to their teaching repertoires the practice of using literature–both fiction and nonfiction–to add depth and interest to their teaching.

While those subject matter areas are relevant and important at appropriate grade levels, the move toward thematic teaching has cast a bit of a shadow over subject matter areas in favor of broader questions and concerns. Themes related to subject matter areas are being replaced in many schools and districts with themes that are more conceptual: communities, change, interactions, movement. To insure student interest, the choice of themes should be jointly planned with students, according to James Beane of the National College of Education in Evanston, Illinois. While his focus is adolescent students, all students should be able to relate to the theme chosen, and it should relate to your grade level requirements (just in case your district is not part of this movement as yet).

The Lend-a-Hand lesson described here incorporates the idea of "relating" and relevancy and proposes that students participate in individual tasks designed to become a collaborative project.

Susan Kovalik, a nationally known education consultant who specializes in thematic teaching, believes that the entire day should be totally thematically integrated and focused on a pervasive theme. Her advice to teachers is that themes be chosen carefully so that they promote future learning, that they have application to the real world, that resource materials are available, and that contrasts and similarities are revealed. A key factor is that the theme relate to other thematic units so that students can learn to make generalizations.

While the lesson that follows does not describe a totally thematically integrated day, it does provide suggestions for combining literature and poetry in a model formulated to create a learning situation where students can "discover" connections. It offers an opportunity for great creativity as well as for concocting a new gestalt. Bringing things together that don't necessarily go together (but have some commonalities) opens students' minds to the larger picture, enhances the possibility for transfer and greater understanding, and certainly adds to one's knowledge base.

The story of the westward movement plays a large part in the study of American history. There are a number of wonderful fiction books recounting the many struggles, but Louise Moeri's unique story, *Save Queen of Sheba*, beautifully describes the courage of a twelve-year-old boy (King David), as he and his little sister (Queen of Sheba), survivors of a Sioux raiding party, struggle to find their parents.

To illustrate the idea of combining literature and poetry in a cooperative venture, a theme must be decided upon. The obvious theme here is that of courage. All of the groups would use the concept of courage for their projects.

GA1494

Each of the four students in each cooperative group is to assume responsibility for one of the following:

1. One group member is to locate two or three paragraphs in the book that illustrate the theme of courage. Copy them and put them in a group folder prepared for this project. The following is an example of a section which might be chosen:

   Slowly King David bent his knees and pulled his feet around to where he could see them. His gray hickory shirt was smeared with dirt and blood–more on the new black woolen britches his ma had made for his twelfth birthday last week, and still more on his left arm where his head had lain. He raised a hand to his chest, his face, his head. Yes, there. High on his forehead was a ragged tear in the skin, and there seemed to be a loose flap of skin with hair on it hanging loose. He could tell there were thick, sticky clots of blood matted in his sandy hair and streaked down his sunburned, bony face.

   "Tried to scalp me," he said aloud in the silence around him, "but didn't quite."

   He could see that several wagons were scattered around–some of them had been burned, but the fires were out now, with only a heavy stinking smell of smoke that was drifting slowly away on the faint breeze. He now felt very thirsty, but it looked as if all the water kegs had been smashed, as well as sacks of flour and beans torn open and spilled on the ground. Slowly, carefully, he tried to stand up, but on the first attempt his head banged and roared and he had to stop. Then he crawled on hands and knees over to the nearest wagon, grasped the wheel in bloody hands, and pulled himself up.[1]

   Got to look around.

   The next step is to prepare to read the chosen selection. Practice with other cooperative group members is essential for this to be a cohesive presentation.

2. Two group members are to locate two poems from any sources which also illustrate the theme of courage. These students may work together or independently in their search, or all four group members may prefer to work on this together. School library personnel may be helpful in this instance, as might classroom aides or parents. Since courage is as much a concept as a word, fully understanding its meaning may require more than a trip to the dictionary, but that trip to the dictionary will also help in locating poems because it offers possibilities. Courage, Webster's states, is "...the attitude of facing and dealing with anything recognized as dangerous, difficult, or painful, instead of withdrawing from it."

---

1.   From SAVE QUEEN OF SHEBA by Louise Moeri. Copyright (c) 1981 by Louise Moeri. Used by permission of Dutton Children's Books, a division of Penguin Books USA Inc.

GA1494

Also a tie-in to history, albeit a little earlier, "Paul Revere's Ride" provides another look at courage. This is the last stanza of Longfellow's epic poem:

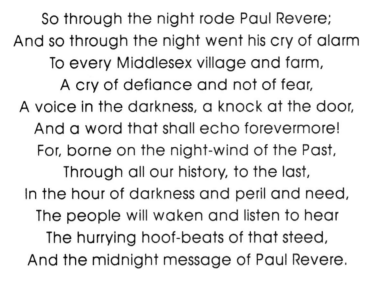

So through the night rode Paul Revere;
And so through the night went his cry of alarm
To every Middlesex village and farm,
A cry of defiance and not of fear,
A voice in the darkness, a knock at the door,
And a word that shall echo forevermore!
For, borne on the night-wind of the Past,
Through all our history, to the last,
In the hour of darkness and peril and need,
The people will waken and listen to hear
The hurrying hoof-beats of that steed,
And the midnight message of Paul Revere.

Here is a second selection, also echoing the theme of courage, also historic and even earlier, the first four stanzas from "The Landing of the Pilgrim Fathers," by Felicia Dorothea Hemans:

The breaking waves dashed high
    On a stern and rock-bound coast,
And the woods, against a stormy sky,
    Their giant branches tossed;

And the heavy night hung dark
    The hills and waters o'er,
When a band of exiles moored their bark
    On the wild New England shore.

Not as the conqueror comes,
    They, the true-hearted came:
Not with the roll of the stirring drums,
    And the trumpet that sings of fame;

Not as the flying come,
    In silence and in fear,
They shook the depths of the desert's gloom
    With their hymns of lofty cheer.

GA1494

3. Each piece of literature will require a short introduction which the cooperative group will prepare together. The fourth group member will assume the role of narrator. The introductions serve to tie the pieces together to illustrate the theme of courage. The introductions to each piece may be read by the narrator, who should also give the title and name of the author prior to the reading of the chosen selections by the appropriate group members. (The narrator may also choose to define the theme word.) The selections (and their introductions) may be read in the order decided upon by the group, then possibly be used to generate bulletin board displays focusing on the themes.

Introduction:

The Pilgrims crossed the ocean to go to a land they knew nothing about. The United States of America began because of the courage of this small group of people. "The Landing of the Pilgrim Fathers" by Felicia Dorothea Hemans.

(Read selection aloud.)

Introduction:

England tried to rule the colonies, and the Revolutionary War began when the British fired on the Minutemen in Lexington, Massachusetts. The colonists wanted their freedom from British rule. It took courage to ride through the night to warn the Americans that the British were coming. "Paul Revere's Ride" by Henry Wadsworth Longfellow.

(Read selection aloud.)

Introduction:

Courage takes many forms. Pioneers moving across the United States to find new homes had courage. King David was just twelve years old and he needed lots of courage after a raiding party of Sioux Indians killed everyone in the wagon train except him and his little sister, Queen of Sheba. *Save Queen of Sheba* by Louise Moeri.

(Read selection aloud.)

GA1494

If you are using this idea with younger children, a poetry file and suggestions would be appropriate. With adequate time, you might even have poems that older students could choose.

A little "variation on the theme" of themes could incorporate the use of outstanding children's picture books, which often provide a vehicle to help children understand the meaning of such words as courage, perseverance, responsibility, determination, and perspective. Wonderful books like *Old Henry* by Joan W. Blos (Morrow Jr. Books, New York), which deals with acceptance of people who are different, or *Chester's Way* by Kevin Henkes (Puffin Books, New York), which looks at friendship from a unique perspective, are ideal for tying together with poetry. Many picture books are short enough to be read in their entirety instead of in excerpt format.

For you:

1. Choose a theme (because it falls within the parameters of your needs).

For your students:

2. Locate two or three paragraphs in a book that illustrate the theme. Copy them.

3. Go to the library and look through poetry anthologies to find two poems that have the same theme. Copy them.

4. Write an introduction for the book and for the two poems.

5. Write your theme on the cover of a folder. Put your selections inside in the order you like best.

6. Prepare for and plan a presentation to the class. Practice by reading your selections aloud with your group as an audience. Read your selections to the class on your assigned day.

Plan a bulletin board display for your selections!

31

GA1494

Discovering Meanings

The work sheet on the following page is an example of the type of assignment that easily fits into the format of this strategy. Even with a page prepared for a traditional lesson in which one student completes all the items, Lend-a-Hand offers an alternative which increases both teamwork and learning. Each group member should be assigned an equal amount of work. Thus, in this case where there are thirty-two items, each student in a group of four would be responsible for discovering the true meanings behind eight of the idiomatic expressions.

One particularly effective study skill for an exercise such as this one is the use of index cards. Provide each student with eight cards, one for each phrase and its true meaning. Tell your students to write the phrase on one side of the card and its "translation" on the other side. (This works extremely well for new vocabulary words, new terms specific to a unit of study, foreign words, etc.) With this method, students can quiz themselves as well as their teammates. Sufficient time with dictionaries, dictionaries of idioms, and/or E.D. Hirsch's *Dictionary of Cultural Literacy* will help students discover the meanings of the phrases they've been assigned. (You might wish to assign phrases by numbering students: "If you are number one, take phrases 1 through 8.") Time must be allowed for study and for becoming familiar with the phrases. This could be a homework assignment.

Now the fun begins! Students in their cooperative groups are given time to teach the true meanings of the phrases to their teammates. To maintain interest, a good strategy is to have a student teach only one phrase at a time; then have the "teaching" job rotate to the next student.

To ensure that each student in the group has written definitions for each phrase, passing the index cards from person to person within the group will allow all members to copy from one another's cards. All students are accountable for all definitions.

Debriefing your students following an activity such as this one should include some discussion on teaching tips. Asking students what they did to help one another remember meanings may evoke some mention of a mnemonic device or an illustration or example which helped everybody.

GA1494

Say What?

Some words don't mean what they say. What ideas and meanings are really behind these idiomatic expressions?

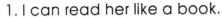

1. I can read her like a book.
2. Don't cross that bridge until you come to it.
3. They'll never say that I passed the buck.
4. She burned the midnight oil.
5. She has butterflies in her stomach.
6. That's a piece of cake.
7. He's burning the candle at both ends.
8. She pulled the carpet out from under him.
9. He let the cat out of the bag.
10. They were playing cat and mouse with him.
11. She hit the ceiling.
12. It's a catch-as-catch-can situation.
13. He has her going around in circles.
14. She took him to the cleaners.
15. Two heads are better than one.
16. They can put two and two together.
17. He's barking up the wrong tree.
18. He said it with tongue in cheek.
19. I am all thumbs.
20. He stole her thunder.
21. It was a real white elephant.
22. It was just sour grapes.
23. You were just knee high to a grasshopper.
24. We're in the gravy now.
25. The grass is greener on the other side of the hill.
26. That's the pot calling the kettle black.
27. He'll be there 'til the cows come home.
28. They're breathing down my neck.
29. It was hard to keep a straight face.
30. He really had egg on his face.
31. It's time to face the music.
32. She had to eat her words.

GA1494

Perspective

Perspective is a unique cooperative strategy because each student in a cooperative group is asked to investigate a literature selection from a different perspective. Looking at familiar literature in new ways and interpreting new readings from an atypical viewpoint builds interest, appreciation, and understanding.

Books not only tell wonderful stories; they open the door for some innovative cross-curricular teaching opportunities. Teachers today frequently use sets of novels in their classrooms to bring a historical period to life. The use of Louise Moeri's *Save Queen of Sheba*, as discussed earlier (see pages 28-30), brings the westward movement alive far more than two paragraphs in a history book could. The history is still necessary, but the fiction brings a deeper appreciation and understanding of the time. In much the same way, the appreciation of literature can be greatly enhanced when there is a more thorough understanding of the history.

Perspective initiates an approach to instruction which requires guided practice sessions for the entire class in the beginning and then cooperative group practice sessions as skills are developed. The purpose of this strategy is to use a fictional selection to teach a wide variety of learning-to-learn skills. *Save Queen of Sheba*, or any other book used for this purpose, should be read solely for pleasure prior to the extensive close examination which is integral to Perspective. The questions you ask may be metaphorical; they may require children to empathize, to compare and contrast, to imagine, and to evaluate. Your students will assume the roles of specialists: a geographer looking at the physical setting to determine how the landscape affected the wagon train and its survivors, an anthropologist empathizing with the Indians, a psychologist discussing courage, a historian comparing fact with fiction.

The perspective taken will depend on your literature selection. Perspectives for older students which might be explored include biologist, botanist, zoologist, oceanographer, historian, geographer, anthropologist, psychologist, or book reviewer (an interesting perspective when one considers that instances of good writing, effective use of imagery and description, as well as interest would be discussed). For younger students, the opportunity to relate to individual characters and to discuss the selection from that character's perspective provides experiences in developing empathy and learning the skills of comparing and contrasting. Additional perspectives for younger students include discussing the setting, the problem or conflict, and the resolution of the story.

Be certain to provide several guided experiences investigating a single perspective as a class, then additional experiences within cooperative groups (four different perspectives within a group, all groups having the same assignment). Once your students have some background in the process and feel comfortable with it, a variation could include having each of the students in the class who have been investigating the same perspective work together for a short period sharing observations. They would leave their cooperative groups and meet in a "job-alike" group—all the book reviewers would meet, all the anthropologists would meet, etc.

After a given time period, the "job-alike" individuals would return to their cooperative groups to enlighten group members. The depth of understanding which evolves promotes group bonding, interest, accountability, and recognized interdependence as information is organized into a network of related facts. Skill teaching within context is epitomized with Perspective as the interpretation and assimilation of new ideas weave together a background for future learnings and greater possibility for transfer.

GA1494

The Lupine Lady

Barbara Cooney's wonderful book, *Miss Rumphius* (Puffin Books, New York) tells the story of Alice Rumphius whose Victorian childhood is beautifully depicted by the author/illustrator in this award-winning book. When Alice tells her grandfather that she wants to travel the world and then live by the sea, he tells her she must also do a third thing–something to make the world more beautiful. The story follows Miss Rumphius on her travels and, when she settles down to her home by the sea, we wait to find out what she decides to do to make the world more beautiful.

The beauty of the illustrations and the way they help the author tell her story would be a unique perspective to take when looking at this book closely. Another perspective would be that of a geographer or travel agent, mapping out the itinerary of Miss Rumphius' travels. Although the places she travels to are unnamed, a little guesswork and imagination would provide interest to this perspective. From a scientific perspective, the lupine could be investigated; from a psychological perspective, Miss Rumphius herself is a most intriguing individual to study.

Questions to ask or assignments to make to elicit different perspectives might include:

If you were a newspaper reporter, what questions would you ask Miss Rumphius when you interviewed her? (What kind of person was she?)

Imagine that you are Miss Rumphius. You have traveled and are ready to settle down in your house by the sea. Write a letter to a friend. (How did she see herself?)

Use a world map to trace Miss Rumphius' travels.

In what ways are you like Miss Rumphius?

Do you agree that Miss Rumphius was a "crazy old lady"? Give reasons.

Use the information in the book and visit the library to give a scientific report on lupines.

Compare Miss Rumphius' childhood with her later life.

How did Barbara Cooney use sensory images to add reality to this story? (What descriptions were given so that you could almost feel, taste, see, hear, and smell?)

Imagine that you are Miss Rumphius and you must choose something to make the world a more beautiful place. What would you choose, and why?

GA1494

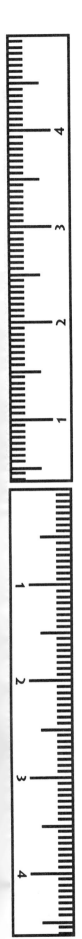
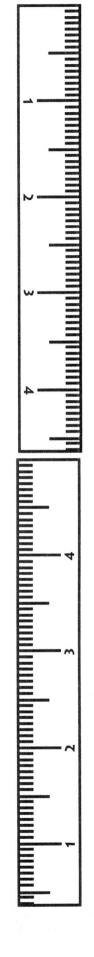

Another option would be to assign the same perspective to each group member, but a different perspective to each group. Time must then be allowed for in-group sharing and whole-class sharing.

For primary children, the perspectives chosen could focus on setting, character, problem/conflict, and resolution. An in-depth look at each of these and in-group discussion, followed by sharing of group findings with the entire class, would be a learning experience for all students.

There is a great emotional appeal in this book for younger and older children, and the perspectives assigned should enrich the reading of the story, not create a tedious exercise. A group assignment for a book such as this one should not be overly long and should be designed to provoke interest and add a more in-depth appreciation. Picture books of this quality appeal to all ages and can be used for a multitude of purposes.

GA1494

Round and Round

This strategy involves a structured writing assignment which may or may not involve creative input, depending on the type of assignment given. Because children will be "piggybacking" on one another's ideas as papers are passed from student to student, **Round and Round** also develops flexibility and critical thinking skills. Ideas are generated as students adapt to each new paper. Round and Round may be used in any area of the curriculum when students are asked to report on a topic, expand on a thought, or respond to a prompt.

Ask each of your students to take out a sheet of paper and a pencil or pen. This assignment may be structured in a variety of ways but is dependent upon a writing prompt: a question, issue, or problem which can be responded to in sentence format. All cooperative group members are to start writing when the prompt is given and continue writing until a predetermined signal is seen or heard. At that signal, each student is to pass his or her paper to another group member (on the left, on the right, or the next number in numerical order) who will continue writing on the sheet passed until the predetermined signal is given again, at which time the students will exchange once more. After everyone has had a chance to add to everyone else's paper, the activity should end with a summary sentence added by the paper's originator.

Without question, this cooperative activity has resulted in some of the most "interesting" end products. Students who enjoy creative thinking exercises will find much to stimulate their thinking with this strategy. Students who have difficulty generating ideas will find inspiration. They are generally eager to share results both within their cooperative groups and with the entire class. Discussion is a must. The concept of ownership may initially be an issue which will concern students, but the fun and humor that the strategy engenders soon overshadows the ownership issue. To take advantage of the humorous aspects of this strategy, a follow-up to this activity could involve the group using their individual/piggybacked products to create a team product.

The examples which follow illustrate the wide-ranging uses of Round and Round.

GA1494

Alexander and the Terrible, Horrible, No Good, Very Bad Day

Literature provides us with an extraordinary means for accessing feelings. Several wonderful children's books have been written by authors sensitive to the multitude of emotions and experiences children share. One of those books is *Alexander and the Terrible, Horrible, No Good, Very Bad Day*. Judith Viorst manages to detail, from a first person perspective, a disappointing and traumatic day in the life of Alexander, a child to whom readers of all ages can relate. Alexander's feelings of mistreatment, outrage, and exasperation mirror the feelings of many children.

Many books serve similar purposes, yet this particular one is being used to illustrate the process because it is also one which will sensitize students to one another's feelings. After reading it to your class, you might wait a day or two; then direct your students in the Round and Round cooperative activity.

Each student will need paper and pencil. Begin by saying:

> Do you remember that terrible, horrible, no good, very bad day Alexander had? What kind of things happened to him? Have you ever had a day like that? Have you ever had a day when everything went wrong? Maybe you had a day when just one very important thing didn't turn out the way you wanted. Maybe you had a day when you were very disappointed. You may have lost something important to you, had a friend move away, had someone get mad at you for no reason, or didn't get to go somewhere you wanted to go. Think about it for a minute or two. When I tell you to begin writing, write one sentence which begins to tell about one event that happened on a terrible, horrible, no good, very bad day of yours.

Allow adequate time for students to get their first thoughts down on paper. Ask them to stop by saying:

> Finish the sentence you are on; then lay your pencils down. You are going to pass your papers to the person on your right. Write another sentence. This time, however, your sentence should make sense with what has already been written on the paper you get. It can still be about something you've experienced, but you are helping now to make up a story like the one we read. Add another sentence which makes sense and continues the story.

Allow time for that second thought. Ask your students to pass their papers and write one more sentence about a very bad day. Continue, with papers rotating, until everyone in the group has had a chance to add to everyone else's paper. When papers return to their original owners, say:

Please read the Round and Round story on your paper. Think of a good summary sentence which would give a good ending to the story on your paper and write it.

These "piggybacked" creations will evoke an abundance of laughter about "bad" experiences, and a growing realization that everyone shares similar experiences.

Ask:

What did you like about this activity? What did you notice about the experiences you and your group have had?

A wonderful follow-up to Round and Round would be the creation of a group or class product utilizing input from the group's responses to the prompt. This could be done in the form of a story or a poem or by using another cooperative strategy.

And Where It Ends, Nobody Knows

Round and Round is a cooperative strategy which provides a slightly divergent means of encouraging creative output. This activity focuses on improving descriptive writing by employing specific parameters in the prompt. To prepare students for writing, spend time discussing imagery and how authors use references to the senses to create scenes which are realistic. Ray Bradbury authored a short story, "The Long Rain," in which description almost surpasses reality, so inundated do we feel by just a few sentences.

If you can locate the short story and share some of the descriptions with your students, do so. Discuss the senses that are involved–that rain can surely be seen, felt, heard, and smelled. Discuss the differences between just saying, "It's raining," and Bradbury's description of the rain on Venus where it hadn't stopped raining for more than a million years. Ask students how Bradbury appeals to the sense of touch. What are the appeals to the senses of sight, smell, and hearing?

Assign a different scene for each of your cooperative groups to create. Four sheets of paper can circulate, building four different scenes; then students can work together to distill the four stories into one.

Ask students to create:

a scene with thunder and lightning	a scene that is hot and dry
a scene with fog	a scene that is dark and damp
a scene with wind	a scene that is green and rainy
a scene that is cold and wet	a scene that is gray and dreary

With a little practice, students can work effectively together to build their image-making skills using reference to the senses. This is a great deal more interesting than a work sheet, as it becomes almost a forced-choice situation which stimulates inventiveness. Be sure to allow time for each group to polish its efforts and share its finished product.

Continue to build awareness of descriptive passages in any literature which is exemplary in that area. By sharing your appreciation of the power of the written word, it becomes an ongoing reminder for your students.

GA1494

Merry-Go-Round

This strategy is primarily a "process" activity; it is not intended to elicit a finished product. It is intended to set the groundwork for discussion and for learning something together as a group. In **Merry-Go-Round** students circulate around the classroom from learning station to learning station to preview tasks, questions, or directions; confer with their cooperative group; then return to the learning station to respond.

Sometimes it is important to have an activity which allows students to get out of their seats and move around while they work. It's usually difficult to structure moving-around activities and learning opportunities so that they occur simultaneously. Merry-Go-Round is a strategy which sets the stage for a learning experience with a difference.

For this activity you will need some poster board or large sheets of paper which may be taped or tacked to the wall or to cupboards in different places around your classroom. These posters are the "learning stations" which direct students to do specific tasks. Students may take notes on the posters' contents before returning to their groups.

At their seats, cooperative groups discuss, reach consensus, and then return to each station to complete the task required. With one student from each cooperative group designated as recorder, responses may frequently be written directly on the poster. This activity makes it clear to your students that their comments are interesting and valued. Students learn that their ideas are acceptable, that they can synthesize ideas and create new ones.

In every subject area where a thoughtful response to a question is required, where opinions are asked for, when creative fluency is desired, when comments and critiques are invited, Merry-Go-Round serves as a unique vehicle for learning.

GA1494

Headlines

Newspapers provide a number of opportunities for reinforcing skills. This Merry-Go-Round lesson focuses on understanding the main idea of a story and gives students practice creating headlines which go with specific newspaper stories. Begin by locating stories which have high interest for your students so they will enjoy reading them. Cut them out of the newspaper and cut off the headline of each story. You'll probably want as many stories as you have cooperative groups.

Tape or glue each story (headline removed) to a piece of tagboard or poster board. Challenge your students to create a headline for each to communicate the story's main idea. When each group has agreed on a headline, they may write it on the poster board or on a sheet of paper that can be attached to the board. Space the posters around the room so that there is freedom of movement and students are not clustered in one small area.

To critically evaluate the headlines, students may discuss all the entries and choose the one they feel most accurately reflects the content of each story. Another class may be invited in to give their opinions as well.

In a reverse of the above format, headlines may be posted (one per poster) and stories may be written cooperatively for each headline. Teaching the five W's and H–who, what, when, where, why, and how of the story–prior to this variation would be wise.

Another newspaper activity which incorporates the attributes of Merry-Go-Round is to label the posters with categories; then have students in their cooperative groups locate stories relevant to each category and affix them to the appropriate poster. Possible categories include sports, weather, government, crime, entertainment, science, health, travel, food, or fashion.

Questions about news articles may be asked, reactions and opinions to news articles may be solicited, students may be asked to generate questions that they would like to ask about the article, and cooperative groups may be asked to devise their own tasks for posters.

Merry-Go-Round is not only involving; it's a "moving" experience.

Proverbs

People everywhere in the world use proverbs. The suggestion which follows incorporates an introduction to proverbs and provides a format for you to use across the curriculum in similar situations when you wish to test comprehension. Because the group must reach consensus before the group's response is recorded, you have more assurance that everyone in the group has some understanding and has participated in discussion.

Use the information on proverbs to set the stage for Merry-Go-Round and for subsequent activities. This may be considered background material for you or your students; it may be duplicated or copied onto a chalkboard.

If you have ever had someone say to you, "A stitch in time saves nine," or comment, "A bird in the hand is worth two in the bush," then you have received advice in the form of a proverb. Proverbs are simply short bits of wisdom that people all over the world have used for thousands of years. Proverbs offer advice and explain how we ought to feel about things that happen to us. They don't lecture or preach long sermons; they sum up in a few well-chosen words what experience has taught. People of different cultures, living thousands of miles apart, often have very similar proverbs-because each proverb is about a problem that occurs frequently in the lives of all human beings. Proverbs are a form of folklore that is essentially universal.

For this activity you will need poster board or large sheets of paper which can be taped or tacked around your classroom. To introduce proverbs to your cooperative groups, choose eight or ten of your favorites from the list on page 45. Write one proverb at the top of each of the sheets of paper. Following the format described in Merry-Go-Round, your students will circulate in their cooperative groups to each of the posters. They will read each proverb, return to their seats to discuss its meaning, reach consensus, and write down their interpretations. This will continue until each group has interpreted all the proverbs. The group's recorder writes the group's opinion directly on each poster or affixes a sheet of paper to the poster. The recorder may change each time.

Select students to read the different interpretations written on the large sheets of paper. During the debriefing, allow time for discussion of the meanings of the proverbs. To stimulate further discussion, ask students if they agreed with the proverb.

Proverbs from Around the World

He who rides the tiger finds it difficult to dismount.

He who stands with his feet on two ships will be drowned.

Eat to live, not live to eat.

Six feet of earth makes all men equal.

If you want to go fast, go the old road.

Little by little grow the bananas.

Two captains sink the ship.

Chickens always come home to roost.

Ice three feet thick isn't frozen in a day.

Young gambler–old beggar.

Where the river is deepest it makes the least noise.

If you climb up a tree, you must climb down that same tree.

Eggs must not quarrel with stones.

A horse that arrives early gets good drinking water.

By trying often, the monkey learns to jump from the tree.

Many a good man is found under a shabby hat.

People who live in glass houses shouldn't throw stones.

It is better to say a hen ran here than that a rooster died here.

The man who is carried on another man's back does not appreciate how far off the town is.

Faults are like a hill; you stand on your own and talk about those of other people.

A stitch in time saves nine.

A stone in the water doesn't comprehend how parched the hill is.

You can force a man to shut his eyes, but you can't make him sleep.

God gives the milk but not the pail.

45

GA1494

Short Circuit

Short Circuit is a written dialogue in journal format between cooperative group members. This cooperative learning variation of journal writing involves two children who will have what is, essentially, a conversation in writing.

Many teachers use journal writing to give children daily writing opportunities to record feelings, make observations, and to increase fluency. A spiral-bound notebook is ideal for this enterprise. Pages, which may be prepared ahead of time, should be divided in half with a vertical line or simply folded in half lengthwise. The owner of the notebook should write his or her comments in the left column and responses in the right. The date should precede any entry, and a line should be skipped between entries. Because each cooperative group member will dialogue with only one other group member on any given day, you may wish to use Short Circuit three days a week as both a "sponge" (a short, meaningful activity to fill a brief time period) and a "bonding" activity.

Set a special time of day for Short Circuit so that it becomes an integral part of your program. You might consider a schedule which has group member one trading journals with group member two on Mondays, with group member three on Wednesdays, and with group member four on Fridays. The children should understand that this is a quiet activity and that all communication must be in writing. Enough time should be allowed for several sentences to be written. No trade should take place until the owner of the journal has first responded to the prompt, question, or topic. While it is not necessary for a topic to always be given, your students may suggest them when you don't.

Comments, critiques, and opinions can be elicited on such disparate subjects as a book just read, a movie recently viewed, an assembly at school, suggestions for the school, ideas for field trips, reactions to a specific activity, etc. Remember to phrase your prompt so that children may comment to one another and not to you, although they should know that you also are part of their audience. One way that teachers can monitor and be part of the audience for students' journal writing is to collect the journals from different groups on different days. With only four journals to review, the heavy burden of reading through thirty or more journals is eliminated. Should you wish to respond to or question anything written, your responses or questions can be written on Post-it™ Notes so that they do not intrude upon your students' writings. Students who wish to share a particular entry with you may be told to fold a page over at the vertical line.

Discuss the importance of caring about one another's journals. No one will treasure these reflections if the notebooks are not written neatly. Respect for the personal property of others should be stressed. As Short Circuit is continued over a period of time, allow opportunities for children to share with the entire class dialogues they particularly enjoyed, changed their minds about, or responses which made them laugh. Short Circuit will provide sparks for future creative writing assignments and will, as an added benefit, give your students firsthand experience in writing dialogue.

GA1494

I Think I'll Move to Australia

Short Circuit is journal writing with a difference. Using the cooperative group setting, sharing dyads (groups of two within the group of four) provides a support group which can have great power for students of all ages. With a specific topic and a stated time limit, your students are provided a forum for a short uninterrupted time to "talk" with one another. When the topic relates to feelings and the prompt is not given in isolation but is given in relation to subject matter or literature, there is a great lessening of anxiety. Responses toward a subject or topic are far less threatening than self-disclosure, so this process acts as a catalyst for helping children learn who they are while they become receptive to learning about one another.

Judith Viorst's book *Alexander and the Terrible, Horrible, No Good, Very Bad Day* is an example of good children's literature to create a prompt which deals with the issues faced by children. Judith Viorst manages to put some humor into the trials Alexander encounters, and you may choose to read the story to your group to set the stage for the Short Circuit activity. After the reading, the written dialogue you generate will be from this prompt:

> Think about a day when nothing seemed to go right. What happened? How did you feel about each event? Did the day ever get straightened out? How? How did you feel about that?

Each group member will write to that prompt and, when finished, will trade his or her journal with only one other designated group member. That student responds to what has been written in the journal, not to the original prompt. Comments may range from sympathy and empathy to suggestions and advice. As the directions state, your prompt should encourage students to comment to each other, each being the audience for the other's thoughts.

It is suggested that a new topic be used each time Short Circuit is part of journal writing. It is important that each group member has a chance to respond to the prompt and to respond to one other group member, but ordinarily there is no need for continued dialogue. You may wish to involve your students in debriefing.

> How did it feel while you were thinking about what to write?
> How do you feel now about what happened that day?
> Is there anyone who would like to share what he or she wrote and how someone responded?

Annie and the Old One

Conversations in writing are a structured way to encourage thinking about feelings. Verbalizing those feelings in writing often can provide a "sponge" activity for the beginning of the school day. If the writing prompt is on the chalkboard or posted somewhere easily seen in the classroom, your students can open their journals and start writing as soon as they are seated at their desks. Post your arrangement for exchanging journals so that your students may write and respond to writing with direction, but without a great deal of supervision.

Annie and the Old One by Miska Miles (Little Brown, 1971) details the loving relationship between Annie and her grandmother, who is going to die. Annie attempts to interrupt the inevitability of her grandmother's death by unraveling a rug being woven. The finished rug is intended to symbolize the end of her grandmother's life. For children in grades three through eight, it can be used to explain the view of life and death in an Indian culture, and it can open the way for children to express their own feelings about loss and about times when they wished everything to stay the same.

Ask:

Has there ever been a time when you wished everything to stay the same, when you wanted time to stand still? Did you try to do something about it?

By using the story as a forum, the sensitive topic of death and loss can be introduced. The question about wanting things to stay the same allows for commentary that can deal with other issues as well. When the children have had time to write and respond, allow time for sharing thoughts verbally.

GA1494

Testwise

Testwise is a cooperative strategy for test takers. It incorporates some key tips for preparing for a test, introduces techniques for review, and establishes methods for preparing for and answering varied types of test questions.

Have you ever noticed that some ideas are easier to accept because the reasoning behind the idea simply makes sense to you? Often, students are told to study for a test and are even given class time to do so, but rarely are those students equipped to study effectively. Since time immemorial, and even with the advent of portfolio assessment, one of the jobs of a student is still to take tests. It makes good sense to teach them test-taking skills.

Instead of a teacher-conducted review of material covered, utilize class time to have your cooperative groups conduct their own reviews. Each student in every group is to be responsible for formulating a predetermined number of questions–whatever you decide is adequate to cover the material. Students are to prepare answers for those questions on separate sheets of paper. After every member of the group has completed that assignment, the group is to reach consensus on the "best" questions, creating a set of questions which represent input from everybody in the group. A recorder writes the group's questions on a sheet of paper, and the answers to the questions can be written on another sheet of paper by a second group member.

All groups are to keep their answer sheets and pass their question sheets to another group. Your students may work together to answer the questions posed by another cooperative group. When all groups have completed the task, Testwise further reinforces the review process by allowing each group to read the correct answers to the group who took "their" test.

GA1494

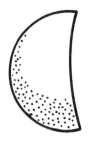

Testing 1, 2, 3...

The purpose of testing is to provide information to both the student and the teacher about the student's learning. Despite the importance of test-taking skills, many of our students do not know how to study for tests. Cooperative groups provide a nonthreatening setting for learning how to study. While the science selection Celestial Snowballs (page 52) is used to illustrate one technique of Testwise, keep in mind that the technique has validity across the curriculum. This approach guides beginning test takers through one simple procedure designed to teach them how to zero in on important information. At the same time, it teaches students how to ask effective questions. In doing so, they are also learning the answers to those questions.

Tell your students that good test takers get ready for a test by trying to figure out what questions will be asked. Have them read a paragraph of the selection within their groups. Celestial Snowballs has a great deal of factual information in it. Point out to your students that each paragraph contains important information, so they should create at least one question for each paragraph. Some paragraphs have a great deal of information and may require more than one question. Tell them that they should each have a total of ten questions of their own, one for each paragraph and four others, before they begin to work in their groups. Suggest that questions and answers be written on separate pages.

Additional suggestions:

Remember that questions begin with the words *who, what, where, when, why, how.*
Ask questions which can't be answered yes or no.
Look for the main idea in each paragraph.
Find out the definitions of words you don't know.
The words *describe, discuss, explain, list, define,* and *compare* are also words which may be used to phrase questions.

When each individual has created ten questions, group members should work together to create a group sheet of the ten "best" questions. Obviously, each group should know the answers to its own questions. Within this structure group members work on consensus-building skills, bonding, and studying as they become testwise. Each group passes its questions to another group who takes the test cooperatively, with a recorder writing group responses.

GA1494

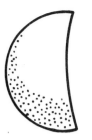

You may wish to use a few questions taken from the various lists to construct your own test. Another thought might be to test each group on its own questions. When this Testwise activity has been completed, and your test has been taken, ask:

How did this type of studying help you?
What did you learn when you worked together to create "best" questions?

Possible Questions for Celestial Snowballs

1. How is a comet described?
2. What kind of orbits do they have?
3. What is perihelion?
4. What do solar winds do?
5. What are the two parts of the head of a comet?
6. What makes a comet look so big?
7. How does the sun influence a comet?
8. How do planets influence a comet?
9. How are meteor showers related to comets?
10. Who thought comets were burning patches of air?

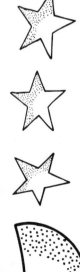

SS2876

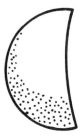

Celestial Snowballs

Bags full of nothing, dirty snowballs traveling on journeys with no end–that's what comets are. These collections of metal and stone, chips, ice, dust, and gases make trillion-mile trips into space and revolve around the sun in elliptical orbits sometimes thousands or millions of years in duration.

As a comet returns from the far reaches of its trip into outer space and approaches perihelion (its closest contact with the sun), the metals melt and turn into gas, and the gases expand forming a larger and larger halo around the comet core. The closer to the sun the comet gets, the more expanded the gaseous halo becomes. It may extend thousands of miles across. The solar winds, a constant stream of particles emitted by the sun, push these gases away from the head of the comet. The gases pushed away from the comet's core form the comet's tail. The tail, forever after, points away from the sun. In its first reunion with the sun and its winds, the tail moves behind the head or over to the side and goes in front of the head as it leaves the sun. As gas in the tail absorbs radiation from the sun, it becomes luminous and glows.

The head of a comet thus consists of a nucleus or center which contains ice, rock, metals, dust, and gases. This part may be only a mile or two wide. This dirty ice nucleus is explained as originating with the formation of the solar system when there were many bits and pieces of ice and dust in space. Around the nucleus is a cloudy covering called the coma. The coma is said to be formed by evaporation of the ice in the nucleus. The nucleus and coma are ususally only a few miles across. It is the tail which accounts for the comet's impressive size, and it is the tail which scientists say could fit into a suitcase (even though it might extend hundreds of millions of miles).

The influence of the sun includes not only the formation of the comet's tail and the comet's speed, but also its color. A comet may be orange, blue, yellow, or green, depending on its distance from the sun. The reflection of the sun's light and the amount of radiation absorbed from the sun also influence the comet's color. The sun has influenced comets for as long as the solar system has existed.

Each time a comet completes its orbit and goes past the sun, material from its nucleus is turned into gas and becomes part of the tail. The nucleus becomes smaller and smaller and though the tail gets larger, the lifetime of a comet is gradually reduced. Even dirty snowballs melt.

We are far more well informed now regarding the makeup of comets than were early comet watchers such as Aristotle. He believed that they were simply patches of air which caught fire and burned. We know they are distant relatives of the sun's family and fascinating to study.

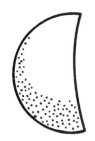

Land of the Rising Sun

The selection entitled "Japan" (page 54) is fairly typical of the dry text-book material which students sometimes encounter. As much as we'd like it, we don't always have exciting resources to teach what must be taught. Studying for a test based on the information in the selection can be made a lot more interesting by employing Testwise strategies.

Because the information is neatly ordered in paragraphs, students in cooperative groups may take turns reading to familiarize themselves with the material. Your role in these initial stages is to review the words which are basic to questioning: *who, what, where, when, why,* and *how*. Additional help could be given by including *explain, name, compare, contrast,* and *list*.

On a paragraph-by-paragraph basis, tell each student to find one or two questions and write them down. When each group member has done so, the group works together to create its own list of the ten "best" questions. The answers to the group's questions are written on a separate sheet.

Possible questions for "Japan"

1. What is Japan's nickname?
2. Who are Japan's nearest neighbors?
3. What body of water is on the east side of Japan?
4. Name Japan's four main islands.
5. What is the capital of Japan?
6. What is Japan's most famous volcano?
7. List three important crops.
8. Name three important industries.
9. Why must Japanese farmers terrace their land?
10. On what island is Japan's capital?

When the questions have been formulated, they are to be given to another group to answer and students may work together on the answers. Groups may correct one another's tests and you may choose to use some of the better questions on your own test.

Debriefing after this kind of involvement should allow for your students to talk about the influence this kind of preparation has on their test-taking skills. To extend learning, you may wish to add some inference-type questions so that some higher level thinking skills will be exercised.

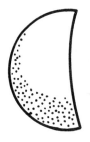

Japan

Far across the Pacific Ocean is the country of Japan. Japan is part of the continent of Asia and is a land so far east of Europe that many Europeans believed it was the end of the earth. Often, we use the words *The Orient* or *The East* to refer to the countries of Asia. It is interesting that the Latin word *oriens* means "direction of the rising sun," and Japan is often called "The Land of the Rising Sun."

Japan is a mountainous country made up of many islands. It is separated from the mainland of Asia by the Sea of Japan. To the east of Japan is the Pacific Ocean. Japan's nearest neighbors are China, Korea, and Siberia. Japan has over three thousand islands, but there are four major islands. They are Hokkaido, Honshu, Shikoku, and Kyushu. Hokkaido is the northernmost island. Honshu is the largest island, has the most people, and the largest cities. Tokyo, the capital of Japan, is on Honshu. Shikoku and Kyushu are southwest of Honshu.

Japan is a land of volcanoes. In fact, it was volcanic action that formed the islands. Hot springs are found throughout Japan because of the underground volcanic activity. There are approximately one hundred fifty volcanoes, but one is the most famous. It is Mount Fuji, over twelve thousand feet high. When it erupted almost three hundred years ago, it covered Tokyo with six inches of volcanic ash. Tokyo is over seventy-five miles away from Mount Fuji.

Because there is so little flat land in Japan, Japanese farmers have learned to create terraces in the mountainsides to plant their crops. Over half of the flat land is used for growing rice. Rice paddies can be seen all over Japan. Other crops include barley, wheat, potatoes, onions, soybeans, tea, tobacco, oranges, and other fruits.

The major industries of Japan include shipbuilding, electronics, heavy machinery, steel, and motor vehicles. Radios, televisions, computers, and automation equipment are also important products. In addition, the Japanese fishing fleet is one of the largest in the world.

Japan is a modern country, though its limited farmland is made up of primarily small farms. The cities are crowded and suffer from pollution. Prices for consumer goods are very high, and travel is very expensive. Because the Japanese cannot produce everything they need and their economy depends heavily on foreign trade, Japan has moved successfully into world markets and has made a great impact. There is little unemployment in Japan and a great deal of hard work.

GA1494

Teams as Teachers

Teams as Teachers places students in the role of teachers and puts them in charge of their own learning. The students in each group number themselves one through four. Each group or team should also have a number. They are given a predetermined amount of time to work with their group to formulate three (or more) questions based on recently studied material. Teams as Teachers is most effective for review and mastery learning of factual information.

To promote organizational skills as well as time management skills, post the allotted preparation time that you are allowing on the board and the clock time at which students must be ready. The questions must have brief answers and be about important information.

Each team must know the answers to its questions.

Each team has an opportunity to be the "teacher." Team 1 is the first teacher, and each member of the team has a specific role to play during the team's tenure as "teacher:"

Person 1 of Team 1 asks one of the questions. Members of each team discuss possible answers, being careful to include everyone on the team.

Person 2 of Team 1 allows a reasonable time to discuss then says, "I call for silence." Then Person 2 calls a number from 1 to 4. All the students with that number (on the other teams) stand up and write the answer on a slate or paper, or are prepared to answer "yes" or "no" in unison, or to give the "thumbs up" or "thumbs down" signal on the count of three.

Person 3 of Team 1 counts down slowly from five to give adequate time for written responses. ("5, 4, 3, 2, 1, stop.") Then Person 3 says, "Hold up your answer."

Person 4 of Team 1 tells each group if they have the correct answer. Teams keep their own scores. Team points may be tallied and be part of a semester-long, team-scoring system.

Teams as Teachers continues until each team has acted as "teacher."

The teacher acts only as a facilitator, so be sure to discuss the "guide on the side" role you will be playing. The responsibility for the success of this process is up to your students. Invite them to formulate reasons why the tactics involved in this strategy constitute a powerful learning tool.

Ask your students what they regard as valuable about the process of formulating questions and "teaching" their classmates. Explain that teaching is a good way to learn, and finding questions to ask also requires learning the answers to those questions.

Motivational quotations are a valuable enhancement to the classroom, and one that fits particularly well here is "To teach is to learn twice," quoted in *No Limits but the Sky* by Susanna Palomares (Innerchoice Publishing, 1992) and attributed to Joseph Joubert. After participating in Teams as Teachers a few times, ask students in their cooperative groups to discuss the meaning of that quote and decide how it directly affects them. A Latin proverb, also in the book mentioned above, "By learning you will teach; by teaching you will learn," adds further support to that viewpoint.

Look! Up in the Sky!

"Reach Out and Touch Someone" is a perfect vehicle for modeling the Team as Teachers strategy because it is filled with factual information which could otherwise be overwhelming and confusing.

You might consider reading paragraphs in numerical order as a way for students within their cooperative groups to become familiar with the information on the handout. Then describe the format for Teams as Teachers by saying:

> You're going to have a chance to work with your group to make up five questions about the information on this sheet. Have a recorder write down the questions. Have someone else in the group write down the answers. Be sure to ask questions which require factual answers, the shorter the answers–the better. Let's number each group and each group member.

Provide adequate time for questions to be formulated. Circulate to make sure groups remain on task.

Team 1 may be the first teacher. Each person on the team has a specific job. Person 1 will ask the questions. Person 2 will say, "I call for silence" and call the number for a member of another team to stand up and be prepared to give the answer. Person 3 will count down from five to give time for written responses, or down from three for an oral response or a signal. Person 4 will check for correct answers.

> Person 1: Once a meteoroid enters earth's atmosphere, what is it called?
> Person 2: I call for silence. All the number 4s, please stand.
> Person 3: On the count of three, all of you tell me in unison what a meteoroid is called once it enters earth's atmosphere. One, two, three. . . .
> Person 4: Meteor is the correct answer.

At this juncture, the strategy offers two options. Team 1 may ask all of its questions using the format above, or each team may have a turn being teachers until all questions are asked. This may be a more desirable way of doing it since duplicate questions will be eliminated and it will be more likely that all teams will have a chance to be teachers.

57

GA1494

Possible Questions for "Reach Out and Touch Someone"

What is another name for a meteor? (shooting star)

What is the name of the spot from which it appears that meteors originate? (the radiant)

What does the suffix *-id* mean? (daughter of)

What falls to earth from shooting stars? (cosmic dust)

What is a meteor called once it hits the earth? (a meteorite)

Summary: After all of the teams' questions have been asked, ask your students:

What did you like about this strategy?

What didn't you like?

What did you learn from being teachers? (Hopefully, someone will express the thought that teaching is a great way of learning.)

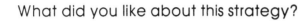

GA1494

Reach Out and Touch Someone

Many years ago, it was believed that meteors were signs of heavenly anger. The gods' messages, it was felt, were sent by way of fireballs–a method of communication with little reliability but great impact.

The feeling then, as now, was that first you had to get your audience to pay attention. Tribal chiefs and foreign princes trembled as meteors streaked across the skies. They worried more about the possibility of impending death than scientific explanations. We shall concern ourselves with scientific explanations.

A meteoroid is a solid object which moves through space at tremendous speed–25 to 30 miles per second. It is often no bigger than the head of a pin or a speck of dust. As it races through space, a bright glowing streak appears, which means that it has come into the earth's atmosphere. This mass of glowing gases is called a meteor. It is one of at least ninety million which are seen to enter our atmosphere daily. Meteors speed only 20 to 70 miles above the earth. They collide with molecules of air, create friction, heat, and then burn. These "shooting stars" produce cosmic dust which falls to earth, several hundred tons of it each day.

Sometimes a meteoroid will reach the ground without completely burning up. It never goes through the meteor stage. It never returns to the dust from whence it came–it hits the ground and is then known as a meteorite. Some meteorites may be comet debris; larger meteorites may be escapees from the asteroid belt between Mars and Jupiter. Some metal is found in all meteorites, which differentiates them from rocks found on the earth's surface, but no new elements have been found in them.

Comets are also thought to be responsible for the atmospheric display known as a meteor shower. A comet's participation involves sharing a bit of itself, even though it's made up of practically nothing. The gravitational pull of a large planet can rip away some of the solid matter in the comet, and the particles, though remaining in cometary orbit, pass through the earth's orbit as they move into our atmosphere. Each trip around the sun also pulls rock and dust particles out of the gaseous cometary matter.

When a meteor shower occurs, it appears that the meteors originated from the same spot–that spot is called the radiant. This is somewhat of an optical illusion as meteors travel in straight lines. It is the earth passing through the meteor swarm, and where you are standing and watching, which creates the illusion. In some meteor showers you can see as many as 50 meteors in an hour. In 1833 one meteor shower had 240,000 meteors in nine hours. There are about a dozen meteor showers each year that occur on about the same date. The radiant of many of these showers appears to be a particular constellation. The meteor shower names all end with the suffix *-id*, which comes from the Greek and means "daughter of." The most well-known are the Perseids, from the constellation Persus, and the Leonids, from the constellation Leo.

GA1494

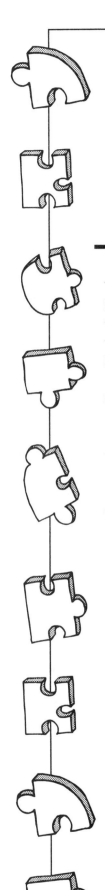

Co-op Connections

Co-op Connections sets the scene for your students to learn to make inferences about their own learning. Hypothesizing in anticipation of what they are going to be studying helps students in cooperative groups think critically as they seek out relationships and create connections. Each group shares its "connections" with the entire class, and discussion helps to formulate concepts and provides an opportunity to synthesize ideas.

This practical strategy can be used or adapted for all grade levels and is relevant in all curricular areas. Its strength is its simplicity and the fun of the process. It builds anticipation for learnings to follow. Co-op Connections is a cooperative activity which trains students to use inductive logic. Approached in stages, this strategy first asks children to work independently and then as a team, with their responses refined as they move through the process.

In every area of the curriculum, there are words that are particularly relevant to a specific unit of study, whether it is history, biology, music, art, or literature. As you begin a new unit of study or as you introduce a literature selection, go over the materials which you will be using with your students and create a list of those words which the children may be encountering for the first time along with other words which are particularly important to the subject being introduced.

Use an overhead projector, chart paper, or a chalkboard to share the list with your students. They may copy it, you may provide copies, or students may work from the projected list. If there are many unfamiliar words, you may wish to allow additional preparatory time for students to use the dictionary or you may wish to engage the class in a discussion of word meanings.

Allow the students to work independently, grouping words together which appear to have common characteristics on a separate sheet of paper. (Groups might include animal words, words about weather, adjectives, things that shine, etc.) A paper folded into fourths works well, with the student's selected classification label at the top of each quadrant. After working independently for a specified period of time, students should share their groupings and work together to create more or to refine their groupings. This final collaboration will elicit less obvious classifications, and students should be encouraged to be creative.

GA1494

Take a Right

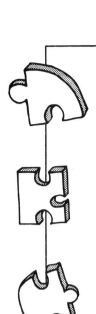

The words listed on the following page have been taken from the selection "Turn Right at the Land Bridge"(page 63). They may be used in a handout, written on the board, or shown on an overhead projector. Because the vocabulary used in this strategy is taken directly from the content information your students will be studying, the process which follows builds in readiness for new subject matter being introduced. This inductive approach to learning offers opportunities for inferential thinking and hypothesizing, both areas of critical thinking which are often given short shrift by designers of curriculum.

To introduce a new unit of study in any subject area, use the words from the text and ask the children to create groupings of words which have common characteristics. As you create the list, choose words which have enough relevance to naturally provide clues for those groupings.

Ask your students to work independently for several minutes. Explain to your students that any reason they decide upon for grouping is acceptable. The group involvement which follows each student's independent efforts extends thinking and moves your students past obvious connections. Ideas for grouping from one student's paper will spark other grouping ideas.

After your students have familiarized themselves with the listed words, you may wish to discuss the possibilities of subgroups and alternative ways of grouping. Most students lack familiarity with this type of learning, so it will affect the ease with which they move into this activity. Different degrees of guidance may be necessary until a comfort level is achieved.

Plan to introduce the actual subject matter reading material after there has been sufficient time to discuss group findings. The relationships discovered and inferred by your students will reinforce the learnings to come and serve also to spark interest in new information. Debrief in this way:

What discoveries did you make by yourself?

What discoveries did you and your group make together?

What were you thinking about during the times you were labeling and categorizing?

What were some of your new ideas?

GA1494

Take a Right

Examine the words below and find groupings of two or more words that are related in some way. Think of a way to describe or label your groupings. After working independently for about ten minutes, work with your cooperative group to create more groupings. Be prepared to explain the classification of each grouping.

hunters

continent

fishermen

wildlife

Alaska

glaciers

land bridge

environments

canoe

wanderers

land

knives

ivory

tools

Asia

North America

Ice Age

mariners

interior

basketry

Arctic

culture

marine mammals

languages

totem poles

stone

sea

ancestors

GA1494

Turn Right at the Land Bridge

During the Ice Age, glaciers held most of the waters of the oceans in a frozen state. As the Ice Age ended more than 15,000 years ago, the ice began to melt and a land bridge formed between Asia and Alaska.

Before the seas rose and water covered that land bridge, hunters from Asia crossed into North America. These Asian hunters were the first to see Alaska and, in fact, were the first to see our continent.

As the hunters wandered from place to place they began to settle into areas which they liked. As they settled in different places, they developed different life-styles. Their life-styles, or ways of life, were directly related to their different environments.

Those who settled along the coast of southeast Alaska had a wealth of seafood, were great canoe and totem pole builders, and were also skilled in basketry. These were the Tlingit, Haida, and Tsimshians. They developed a culture much different from that of the people who roamed further inland and settled there.

The Athapascans occupied the interior Arctic areas. They fished for salmon, but spent more time hunting for moose, caribou, bears, and other wildlife. They had few arts because they spent so much time moving about, but they did make knives of stone and copper.

Other groups settled along the north and west coasts and islands of Alaska. Those who settled in the southwest were the Yup'ik and in the far north, the Inupiat. The people who lived on the Aleutian Islands were called Aleuts. Aleuts were very skilled at basketry and were expert mariners. Some craftspeople learned how to carve ivory into tools, utensils, and ornaments. The sea was very important to all of the people who settled on the coast.

There are native Alaskans who still live much the same as their ancestors did and many who have changed and adapted their life-style to more modern ways.

Developing a Thinking, Meaning-Centered Curriculum

Enrichment teaching used to be considered the province of teachers of the gifted, but a vast amount of research is providing evidence that with "enrichment," gifted behaviors can be developed in a much larger population than that delimited by IQ scores. The national movement towards school restructuring has led researchers to look at educational change in general, and specifically has focused on the success of "gifted" activities in the regular classroom. Having taught cluster groups of gifted students within a regular classroom setting for several years, my experience has been that all students profit from the process-oriented, thinking skills-based activities designated "gifted."

Dr. Joseph Renzulli and Dr. Sally Reis, both of the University of Connecticut, authored a study, "The Schoolwide Enrichment Model," which focused on strategies previously used for gifted students. They believe that integrating thinking processes into the regular curriculum should be done whenever possible. They have concluded that all teachers should be involved in "enrichment teaching" and that educational change can occur only if there is less emphasis on drill and practice and more on providing challenging experiences for our students.

One of the issues discussed in the research studies was the need for focusing on practical ways in which the classroom teacher can integrate process skills into the regular curriculum. Intriguingly, serendipitously, but not surprisingly, the core of what has been suggested reflects all that is wonderful in cooperative learning: small group investigations and curriculum extensions. School performance related to attention span, attention to detail, motivation, and study skills are all affected positively when a thinking, meaning-centered curriculum is in place.

The next several pages reflect the research related to creating meaning from curriculum content, and they give a sampling of the ways in which teachers can "enrich" their classrooms. There are seven general methods suggested.

- Participating in active, challenging, attention-holding experiences
- Putting thoughts into words
- Using real-life experiences and primary source materials
- Creating real products to show understanding of the whole and its parts
- Using the methods, processes, and vocabularies specific to subject content areas
- Applying skills and concepts across subject matter boundaries to better understand content
- Participating in activities that relate personal ideals and values to subject matter, to be involved in reasoned ethics-related decision-making

GA1494

Participating in Active, Challenging, Attention-Holding Experiences:
Take a Long Walk

Building geographic understandings is a lot more fun outside. A textbook presentation on the fundamental themes of geography can't match the excitement of using your local neighborhood or community as a field laboratory. The opportunity to "see" geography by taking a cultural geography walking tour introduces not only awareness of geographical themes but provides a sound foundation for future learning.

The focus of this walking tour is cultural geography, so the spotlight is not so much on landforms and surface features as it is on inhabitants and land use. A subsequent walking tour to extend learning might focus on the physical features of the area. Classroom preparation for this field trip could involve group assignments which would be completed when students return to the classroom. While on the walking tour, use clipboards and notebooks for note-taking.

Your objectives will vary depending on the grade level of your students, but modeling careful observation and asking questions which require both facts and conjecture will enhance the experience. If parents or classroom aides are available, you might consider some "scripted" preparation and have students remain in small groups with adult supervision. Advance notice of this departure from "normal procedure" should include a reminder to your students to wear comfortable walking shoes. Care should be taken in planning your route so that you are gone no longer than an hour or an hour-and-a-half.

Just as literature has themes, so too do neighborhoods and communities. The themes found in neighborhoods are influenced by the people who have lived there, the people who have moved there, and the way the land is used. The five themes of geography–location, place, human/environment interactions, movement, and regions–can all be related to your area. You might wish to take several short walks, following your initial meanderings, to focus on the following questions related to geographical themes:

Where is our community located? Where is our school neighborhood located in relation to the community?

What physical characteristics in our community's environment have influenced people so that it makes our community different from other communities?

How has property been used in this community? How are buildings used? How have their uses changed?

GA1494

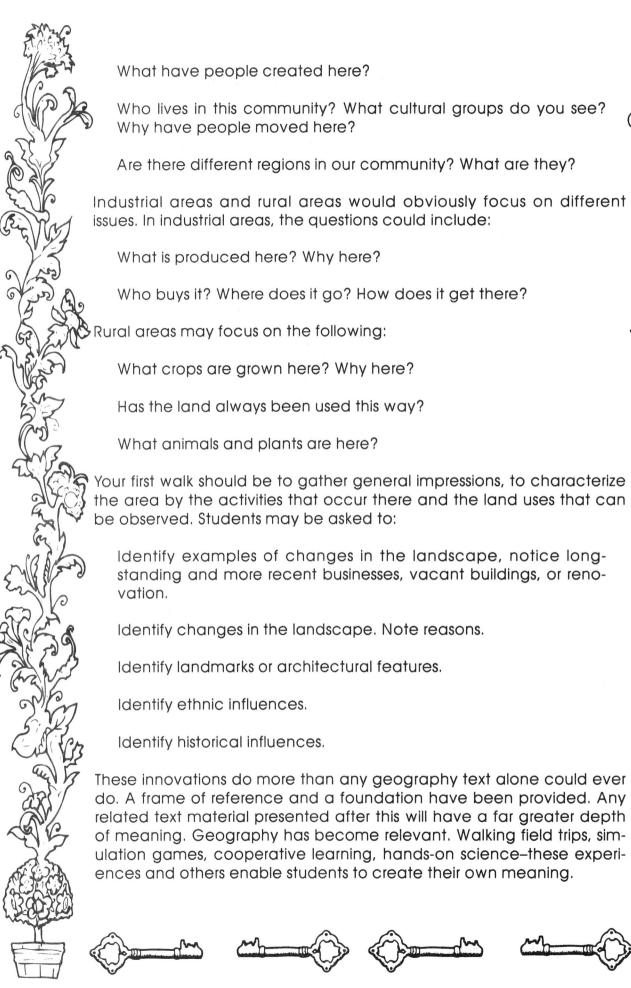

What have people created here?

Who lives in this community? What cultural groups do you see? Why have people moved here?

Are there different regions in our community? What are they?

Industrial areas and rural areas would obviously focus on different issues. In industrial areas, the questions could include:

What is produced here? Why here?

Who buys it? Where does it go? How does it get there?

Rural areas may focus on the following:

What crops are grown here? Why here?

Has the land always been used this way?

What animals and plants are here?

Your first walk should be to gather general impressions, to characterize the area by the activities that occur there and the land uses that can be observed. Students may be asked to:

Identify examples of changes in the landscape, notice long-standing and more recent businesses, vacant buildings, or renovation.

Identify changes in the landscape. Note reasons.

Identify landmarks or architectural features.

Identify ethnic influences.

Identify historical influences.

These innovations do more than any geography text alone could ever do. A frame of reference and a foundation have been provided. Any related text material presented after this will have a far greater depth of meaning. Geography has become relevant. Walking field trips, simulation games, cooperative learning, hands-on science–these experiences and others enable students to create their own meaning.

GA1494

Putting Thoughts into Words:
Writing as a Process

Writing instruction in classrooms across the nation has been undergoing a complete metamorphosis. As part of the "writing as a process" movement, the pundits conclude that clear thinking and clear writing are inextricably related. We knew that! In terms of the writing process, however, the stages of prewriting, planning, composing, discussing, revising, and editing are considered necessities. The finished product is just one more step in the "process" and is subsequently given equal treatment and yet far less emphasis than in traditional classrooms.

Many of the cooperative learning strategies detailed in *Cooperative Learning and Motivation* and *Cooperative Learning and Communication* are based on the tenets of whole language philosophy and incorporate "writing as a process" components. The lesson idea which follows is based on the prewriting strategy of clustering. Clustering was originally developed as a writing warm-up exercise to generate a network of thoughts from a nucleus word. It is a type of brainstorming which accesses the right brain's image-making and synthesis capabilities so that words are generated which eventually evolve into a pattern of ideas. Each response generates further responses, all related to the whole.

When students are familiar with the process, a cooperative group cluster can produce a unique group product which forms the basis for writing across the curriculum, studying for tests, outlining, and organizing and sequencing one's thoughts. When done on a group basis, more experiences are tapped into, motivation is increased, the language bank is often added to, new thinking is initiated, and imagination is stimulated. Group clustering convinces students that they do have something to say.

Demonstrate the process by writing a word on the board and drawing a circle around it. Words that reflect common experiences or touch emotions are excellent ways to begin teaching clustering. Words as diverse as *teddy bear*, *breakfast*, *babies*, *pizza*, or *friends* will encourage a free flow of thoughts.

GA1494

Having friends and being a valued friend are important to every child. Many wonderful children's books have been written on the topic of friendship because friends help children relate to their world. Friends provide acceptance and trust. Children often define their own worth in terms of their friendships. Certainly, they have problems with friends, and every child has an ideal "best friend" who sometimes disappoints him or her.

This lesson uses the book *We Are Best Friends* by Aliki (William Morrow & Co., Inc., 1982). It may be used to set the stage and stimulate thinking in primary grade children for this cooperative learning variation of clustering. While the book focuses on a friend who has moved away, the loneliness which follows, and making a new friend, it is the kindling of thoughts about friends which is the key to what unfolds. Read the story to your class; then put the words *best friend* on the chalkboard or on a large sheet of butcher paper and draw a circle around them. Ask:

What kinds of things do you think of when you hear or see *best friend*?

As the children respond, write their responses around the words *best friend*, circling each word or phrase and attaching it with a line drawn to the topic word. Elicit as many responses as possible, asking questions to encourage elaboration. This period should last only two or three minutes. The cluster may be copied and added to within cooperative groups by children who may want to add personal reminiscences. The clustering activity provides the basic ideas for individual stories, a group story, or thoughts for further discussion.

After everyone in each group has had adequate time to contribute to the cluster, the next step is to have the children use the group product to create individual ones. Many times, when we ask children to write, we forget that they often think they have nothing to write about. Because of the emotional responses which clusters evoke, this strategy orchestrates a way for children to write about their thoughts and feelings, a form of expression which may be denied (for a variety of reasons) in many traditional classrooms. Having feelings is a "given," but often children are reluctant to write or talk about them.

GA1494

Using Real-Life Experiences and Primary Source Materials:
Telling Historical Stories

The use of historical fiction to enhance the study of history has been discussed far more than the use of primary source material. The use of primary source material to connect students in a more personal way to history is a strategy which allows them to see the events they are studying through the eyes of someone who was actually there. Primary source materials come from those people who witnessed the actual events. Diaries, letters, photographs, some newspaper articles, some interviews, and memoirs are examples of primary sources. Many social studies texts now incorporate primary source materials to enrich the learning experience.

Primary sources can be used to help students better visualize the physical experiences and emotional reactions recorded by witnesses and recognize that there are stories in history which can be related to their own lives. This lesson sets the stage for using primary sources to begin to teach storytelling skills. By using a combination of primary and secondary source materials (such as history texts, related articles, or the encyclopedia), your students can first gather information which places the story within its historical context in a framework of time, place, and perspective.

"Entering the story from the inside" is how storytellers describe the process of using first-person accounts. Lillian Schlissel's book *Women's Diaries of the Westward Journey* (Schachen Books, 1982) is an excellent example of secondary source material which incorporates primary sources. Without editorializing, Schlissel allows the letters and diaries of over one hundred women to tell their own stories as they give great insight into the tribulations experienced by early travelers on the Overland Trail. To prepare for the storytelling to follow, a student should read some of the selections from the diaries and choose one of the women whose writings touch a chord.

Have students compose questions they might ask of the writer: What emotions was she feeling when she wrote? Why did events occur as they did? How did the writer feel about what happened? Help students personalize this literature encounter as much as possible. They should, in addition, write about their own emotional responses to what they've read. For students to connect primary source real-life experiences to their own lives, they must know enough to empathize with the character and the situation. The student storyteller needs to see the story's sights in his or her mind's eye and feel the character's feelings.

GA1494

Establishing the setting might require further research. There are a number of secondary sources, among them the varied sets of Time-Life books, which feature excellent historical pictures and artwork. Schlissel's book, however, has excellent photographs which certainly set the scene. In addition to setting, students recounting historical stories need to know the order of events as they occurred. Giving the telling an "I was there" quality requires almost a news reporter's demeanor.

There are a number of books which give, in far greater detail, the steps involved in storytelling. To learn the story well enough to tell it to others, mnemonic drawings or key words may be used as cues. Rehearsing, with the cooperative group as an audience, may include opportunities to receive feedback. There are storyteller's recordings available which provide subtle clues as to how to tell a story most effectively. Storytelling as a classroom activity is a viable way to connect primary source materials to your students' lives.

Historical storytelling improves communication skills, reinforces history, teaches about patterns of events, develops appreciation for cause and effect, and provides structured opportunities for students to informatively interpret the meaning of events with another's voice. It is this last advantage which truly forges the link and establishes the connection to personal meaning.

GA1494

Creating Real Products to Show Conceptual Understanding of the Whole and Its Parts:
Abel's Island

William Steig's book *Abel's Island* (McGraw Hill Ryerson Ltd., 1977) captures the imagination in a number of ways, but it took on a new dimension when I discovered that it was also the perfect vehicle for a geography unit. We were finishing the literature-related study of the book and discussing the island which Abel, the delightful mouse protagonist, had made his temporary home, when I asked my students the following question:

> What would it be like to have your own island? What would it look like? Where would it be?

Students talked about it in their cooperative groups, and we talked about it as a whole class. It was a fantasy exercise that became almost real. It became "almost" real because we did create islands; they just weren't real islands. Each student created a salt and flour relief map of an island. Students were required to construct the maps with certain geographic features. They were required to plan for those features by designing a map to scale (or a reasonable facsimile thereof) on graph paper and re-creating it in salt and flour.

I required that ten geographic features be incorporated. That became a powerful aid to teaching the meaning of such formerly abstract terms as *peninsula, butte, mesa, river, lake, strait, canal, bay, cover, fjord, floodplain, estuary, lowlands,* and *channel*. Creating the topographic features of each island required understanding each of the terms, which involved some dictionary investigation and some research. Paying close attention to the exact locations of geographic features and to their impact on the terrain produced intense concentration tempered by the fun of "creating."

When the islands were finished and painted, students located small models of settlements and features that made the islands uniquely "theirs." They discussed economic and agricultural uses of the land, though most preferred their islands pristine and unspoiled. We returned to language arts, creating stories about the islands' histories and inhabitants. Had we taken the time, this probably could have become a civics lesson; there was no doubt that they wanted laws to protect their islands. Families were invited to class as a culminating activity. We spent an entire afternoon welcoming our guests and taking them on a tour of our classroom archipelago.

GA1494

Making a Salt and Flour Map

The Base   Have the lumberyard cut sheets of plywood into twelve-by-twelve inch (30.48 x 30.48 cm) squares. The twelve-by-twelve size would be minimal for this project.

The Map   Have students cover the undersides of their maps with pencil rubbings. Turning the maps right-side up, pressing hard on the top, and going over the outlined shapes of the islands, they can transfer the basic shapes and the locations of the major features to the plywood.

Nails   Hills and mountain ranges can be outlined on the maps with rims of nails hammered in. (This may be more elaborate than necessary, but it also helps to build up the height required for mountains.)

The Goop   Combine three parts salt with one part flour and enough water to create a dough-like consistency. Students may bring the salt and flour, estimating what is needed. Mixing it all up in double thicknesses of plastic bags works well, with students "mixing" by squeezing the bags. The students may do their own measuring and mixing; the amount of finished mixture needed is determined by trial and error and mixed on an "as needed" basis.

First   Cover the entire island area with a thin film of the mixture. Gradually build up the land areas a layer at a time. Each new layer of the mixture should be applied only after earlier layers have had the opportunity to dry. A knife edge or a pencil may be used to trace rivers and locate other features below ground level so their outlines remain visible as the salt and flour layers build up.

Colors   Water-based paints may be used after the islands dry. Traditional color coding reinforces map learning: blue for oceans and rivers (paint directly on the plywood for the surrounding ocean), green for interior lowlands, yellow for desert or coastal sand areas, and brown for mountains.

Additional Activities

Create a small compass rose on the map.

Create questions about the island, using cardinal directions. (What is northwest of the pond?)

Give directions using cardinal directions.

Write letters–one island inhabitant to another.

Engage in trade. Discuss the island's economic resources.

Learn about climate. Study latitude and longitude and their effect on weather.

Create a stamp for the island. Why is its design appropriate?

Create a map of the island and a legend for the map.

GA1494

Using the Methods, Processes, and Vocabulary Specific to Subject Content Areas: The "Hands-On" Approach

The terminology and methodology of the various disciplines have made their way into kindergarten classrooms as well as high school classrooms. Although mathematics, language arts, and the social sciences have their vocabularies and protocols, it is perhaps the natural sciences which have influenced teaching in the most diverse and profound ways.

The science curriculum involves learning vast numbers of vocabulary words, distinctive methods, and innumerable concepts. Maintaining credibility and continuing to grow in popularity as it crosses subject matter boundaries is the "hands-on" approach–formerly limited to science but now widely used in math (with manipulatives), the social sciences, and language arts (through simulations).

The "hands-on" approach is integral to the scientific method, direct involvement being the key to creating meaning. Since science is also a subject that easily lends itself to interdisciplinary activities, the literature connections, writing possibilities, historical investigations, and arts opportunities provide a kind of "double whammy."

A thematic unit based on water can provide several weeks of incredibly divergent "hands-on" activities. Studies of surface tension lead to experimentation with bubbles, poetry writing, and measuring liquids. The desktop provides a flat surface for experimenting with bubbles and the variations that are produced by adding glycerine or liquid dish soap to the bubble liquid. Students use straws to blow into the solutions on their desks and create light-refracting prisms as they learn more about the physical properties of liquids and the geometric shapes that bubble liquids can assume.

When you are done with this unit, you will have the cleanest desks in the school district as well as a collection of the rustiest paper clips. (What else do you use to raise the level of water in a glass, bit by bit?) The prismatic effect of the bubbles will take you on a brief walk into chromatography. Experimenting with paper towels cut into strips, the students use water soluble pens (each choose one color for the experiment) to color a solid design about an inch from the end of a towel strip. With about one-half inch of water in the bottom of the glass, put the end of the towel strip (without the design) into the glass and allow it to absorb enough water to reach the ink. Once the towel strips have absorbed the water, the students take them outside to dry. The results allow the students to hypothesize about "What are we really seeing when we see color?"

There is no doubt that new vocabulary is introduced: *surface tension, tetrahedrons, chromatography, refraction, physical properties, variables, soluble, absorption,* and *prism* are but a few. While your methods may not always be "scientific," they will be "hands-on." It is the students' own experiences, the opportunities to develop their own concepts, to test their own theories, and have a wide variety of examples that result in a high degree of learning. Perhaps the most valuable lesson that "hands-on" activities teach is to remind us, as teachers, that the experiences we provide which stimulate our students to **ask** questions are far more powerful than experiences which require them solely to answer questions.

GA1494

Applying Skills and Concepts Across Subject Matter Boundaries to Better Understand Content:
Across Boundaries

Madeline Hunter is best known for developing the educational methodology known as clinical supervision. The purpose of clinical supervision is to provide a recipe for the development of teaching skills. A major component of that methodology is teaching for transfer. Her explanation of transfer theory has application to all teachers at all levels, regardless of whether or not one subscribes to all that clinical supervision proposes.

According to Dr. Hunter, transfer refers to something in the past that is activated into the present; it can either assist or interfere with learning. Teachers who can "hook" students by connecting new learnings to something they already know that is similar are working to promote transfer. She presents two reasons why transfer is particularly important: (1) it decreases learning time; (2) it is the core of creativity, which affects both problem solving and decision making.

She suggests that identifying and mentally labelling similarities are essential to successful transfer. While children may frequently make their own connections, Dr. Hunter says it doesn't matter who makes the connection, just as long as it is made. Although this is contrary to some theorists who believe that students should be led to make these discoveries for themselves, the basic concept remains the same. I believe that there are situations in which children will "discover" connections themselves. Situations that include a little more "guidance" toward discovery ensure that the connection is made.

Besides assisting students in identifying similarities, provide an abundance of examples when a concept is taught. To give just one example of a new concept is relatively useless. The more examples given, the more transfer is possible. Varied examples should include the students' own experiences and examples of what the concept is not. Its essence should be clear, not ambiguous.

How does this "transfer" to actual and practical classroom use work?

The following lesson on "Similes, Comic and Otherwise" illustrates this application.

74 GA1494

Similes, Comic and Otherwise

When most students attempt to write similes, the results are fairly pedestrian. The thought processes involved in thinking of comparisons require more sophisticated thinking, in most cases, than students are accustomed to. Often, the only experience students have with similes (and metaphors) is irrelevant to anything else that is being learned and involves only recognition and labeling, rarely creating. When they have an opportunity to create, the end result is usually unsuccessful because the preparatory work is so complicated.

This classroom strategy should create some interesting and even humorous similes, with every student able to be successful. It will also be a memorable learning experience in that you are teaching for transfer. When this lesson is over, you can be sure that all of Dr. Hunter's requirements will have been met for a lesson which activates past experiences, provides examples which are "hooks" for new learning, and sets the stage for opportunities to "discover" connections. It can be adjusted to accommodate many different subject areas. In this case, for purposes of illustration, we'll assume that you've just completed a unit of study on Greek gods and goddesses.

Tack ten large pieces of poster board or newsprint in various places around your classroom. At the top of each piece of poster board, write an abstract word such as *Happiness, Fun, Education, Music, Friendship, The Future, Life, Homework, Democracy,* or *Vacations.*

Have students circulate (independently or in their cooperative groups) and think up descriptive words and phrases which reflect their opinions about each of the abstract words. They should write these words and phrases directly on the posters.

You will need to write the names of at least ten (more will provide some choices) of the following gods or goddesses on the board: Zeus, Poseidon, Demeter, Hades, Ares, Aphrodite, Hermes, Artemis, Athena, Hephaestus, Hestia, and Apollo.

GA1494

The task now is for students to write similes combining one of the abstract words from the poster with any of the gods or goddesses on the board. Students may wish to take another look at the posters to decide which descriptive phrases they should use in this "marriage" before they create a cumulative sentence using the abstract word on the chart, the name of a god or goddess, and a descriptive phrase from the chart in this format:

(abstract poster word) is like (god/goddess concrete word)

(descriptive word or phrase describing how, using words from poster).

It should go somewhat like the following:

Vacations are like Hermes; they go by fast.

Homework is like Hades–punishment.

Life is like Aphrodite–lovely and beautiful.

This works particularly well as a cooperative activity because it is far less stressful to collaborate when one is completing an assignment with an unfamiliar format. Creating combinations that seem to have nothing in common is almost "forced association" or synectics. Your students will really need to work at it to make similes, but the effort will create some outstanding results, and "simile awareness" will have occurred, along with transfer. Follow this up with group or individual stories which include the use of the created similes.

Feel free to adjust this lesson to fit your needs. The formula format, which you may also wish to change, works well. You may want to have a guided discussion of descriptive phrases, or include a homework assignment to explore appropriate adjectives for each of the poster words. The concept is easily transferable to many content areas to bring in key words and understandings while enriching language.

GA1494

Participating in Activities to Personally Relate Ideals and Values to Subject Matter, to be Involved in Reasoned, Ethics-Related Decision-Making:
Personal Connections

This expanded Short Circuit activity beautifully illustrates how meaning can be created for children and how they can connect themselves to curriculum content. For two children to have a conversation in writing, the subject or topic to be written about must involve the emotions in some way. This cooperative activity, which works its way around the group in different combinations of dyads, suggests topics which are thematically related to good children's literature. While literature is the specific focus here, this conversational journal writing can incorporate responses to subject matter being studied in a variety of content areas. Personal reactions to historical events, responses to biographies, comments on the implications of scientific discoveries–all are examples of active involvement.

Some of the topics suggested below are followed by titles of books which may be read to the entire class prior to the actual journal assignment. These titles are noted either *primary* or *intermediate* to indicate their most appropriate use. It should be reiterated that there are wonderful, award-winning picture books which delight older students as well as younger students. Frequently, the lessons to be learned are simply stated and provide ready-made writing prompts. There are other wonderful books which will give you further ideas of your own. This list is just a jumping-off point for connecting children to literature and to their feelings.

Have you ever felt you were right about something and no one agreed with you? Did you feel the need to prove that you were right? What did you do? (*The Gift*, Joan Lowery Nixon, intermediate)

Have you ever stood up for something you thought was right even though a lot of people got mad at you?

If you knew by practicing hard you would become the best in your school at something, what would you work on? (*Be a Perfect Person in Just Three Days*, Stephen Manes, intermediate)

If you were given $1000 to use to help other people, how would you spend it? (*The Seventeenth Swap*, Eloise McGraw, intermediate)

If you could live someone else's life for just one week, would you? Who would you choose? (*The One in the Middle Is the Green Kangaroo*, Judy Blume, intermediate)

GA1494

If you had to live with another family for two years, who would you choose? (*Hello, My Name Is Scrambled Eggs*, Jamie Gilson, intermediate)

If you could select only one food to eat, but you could have as much of it as you wanted for the next week, what would you pick? Why?

What do you think is the most unfair thing about the way your family is run? (*Lily and the Runaway Baby*, Susan Shreve, intermediate: *Alexander and the Terrible, Horrible, No Good, Very Bad Day*, Judith Viorst, primary)

What were some of your favorite things to do when you were little? (*When I Was Young in the Mountains*, Cynthia Rylant, primary)

Who would you like to get a letter from? Why?

Think of a time when you met someone you thought was too different from you to be your friend. Did you get to know and like that person in spite of the differences? (*Old Henry*, Joan W. Blos, primary and intermediate)

Do you think boys or girls have it easier? Explain.

What are the biggest differences between what you see on television and what happens in the real world?

What would be the advantages or disadvantages of having an identical twin?

What talent would you like to have? What would you do with it? (*Lentil*, Robert McCloskey, primary)

If you had to give yourself a nickname because of something wonderful that you'd done, what would it be? Why? (*Miss Rumphius*, Barbara Cooney, primary and intermediate)

What was your favorite hiding place when you were little? How did you feel when you were hiding there?

When you think about things that you wish would happen in the future, what are they?

Did you ever have a dream that seemed so real that you thought it had really happened? (*The Magic Honey Jar*, Susi Bohdal, primary)

A component necessary to successful journal conversations using the cooperative learning strategy Short Circuit is a well-phrased question based on a student's previous experience. Children can write about what they know, so background and some emotional involvement work together to provide the material for self-expression.

GA1494

A Look at Multiple Intelligences

The woods would be very silent if only those birds sang who sing the best.

Maximizing student learning should be a goal shared by all teachers. For that reason, the work of Howard Gardner at Harvard University has great relevance. The educational implications of Dr. Gardner's work relate to his theory of multiple intelligences. In a nutshell, Dr. Gardner has identified at least seven kinds of intelligence which translate to seven methods which students have of processing information. While most students are capable of processing information to some degree in all seven modes, student strength is generally seen in a specific intelligence profile.

Because of the distinct characteristics of each of the intelligences, there are teaching methods which obviously will work better with some students than with others. It is, perhaps, awareness of the different intelligences which can help us the most. We are simply not going to have all linguistically intelligent students nor all musically intelligent students in the same classroom. Our classrooms will continue to reflect students with diverse strengths and we need to teach them. Since most schools have traditionally emphasized learning related to only the linguistic and logical-mathematical intelligences, we need to take a closer look at the characteristics of each and then consider the ramifications.

Linguistic students have highly-developed auditory skills and enjoy reading, writing, and using language. They like to play word games, hear and tell stories, and use dialogue. They have well-developed vocabularies, and have a good memory for names, dates, and places. They appreciate humor. They are expressive with language and use it fluently. These are frequently the children whose hands are waving because they know the answers.

Logical-Mathematical students enjoy exploring patterns and relationships and prefer doing their work in a sequential order. They enjoy opportunities to problem solve, to reason, to use logic, to experiment to test what they don't understand, and, unsurprisingly, they generally like mathematics. Analyzing, reasoning, and proving are their most preferred modes.

Intrapersonal students have a deep sense of self-confidence, show early independence, and have a strong will. They prefer their inner world, enjoy being alone, and are aware of their strengths, weaknesses, and feelings. Independent study projects motivate these students. Journal writing and reflection intrigue them.

Visual-Spatial students are able to visualize clear images and pictures when thinking. They are the students who truly can "picture" something in their minds. They can create mind maps related to what they are reading; they enjoy art activities and solving art-related problems, jigsaw puzzles being a simple example. They are comfortable reading and creating posters, maps, charts, and diagrams.

GA1494

Musical students appreciate the sounds of the world around them. They are sensitive to the clamor and clatter of their environment and often enjoy listening to music when they're studying. They have an awareness of pitch, rhythm, and timbre and you may catch them singing to themselves. Rhymes and raps hold great appeal.

Bodily-Kinesthetic students process the knowledge they acquire through bodily sensations and need opportunities to move and to act things out. We often recognize their physical skills during outdoor activities, but the classroom that provides physical activities and hands-on learning experiences such as role play, drama, and games will enhance learning for these students.

Interpersonal students like people. They have many friends and are very "social." They enjoy learning when they can relate to others and particularly appreciate collaborative experiences such as paired learning and cooperative learning. These students have the ability to express empathy for the feelings of others. They see value in cooperation and like competitive experiences.

You have probably already pictured in your mind (if you're even a little bit spatial) specific students who fit the above descriptions. While there will always be some crossing-over, some combining, and some dual strengths, there are good reasons to take this information into our fund of useful knowledge to help us be better teachers.

As you perfect thematic units in your curriculum and provide interactive activities for your students, you can plan for all their needs. Instructional strategies can be designed to address all seven of the intelligences to ensure that your students' differing needs are met. There are methods that can tap into all the intelligences, and options can be provided for completing tasks.

If we focus on individual student growth, we must choose the best methods for reaching each student. Certainly, this does not mean separate lesson plans, but it does mean that we'll rethink the approach we use. The process of learning must become the means by which we build student skills. Teaching methods that relate to the students' dominant intelligences should also help develop capabilities in the others. Essentially, this is personalizing education.

Dr. Gardner's work is continually enhanced and added to by other brain researchers. Additionally, the work related to learning styles has incredible significance. All of it is germane to educating children to love learning. Read on to learn about learning styles and other research, and to discover the way to adapt these findings to your classroom.

GA1494

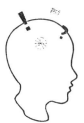

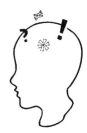

Learning Styles

More than fifty years ago, the Swiss psychologist Carl Jung studied the similarities and differences in the ways the human mind perceives the world and the way it makes judgments based on what it perceives. Jung's findings have influenced current educational practices because they also describe the ways teachers and learners function. Simply put, Jung believed that there were two ways to perceive: sensing and intuition. All of us perceive our world in both ways, but our preference for one or the other dictates how we judge it.

Of the two, sensing is the most concrete. The sensing individual depends upon his or her senses for facts and details. Direct experience is the sensing individual's reality. It is fixed. Sensing individuals are practical; they enjoy routine, they work hard and they expect results. On the other hand, intuition is abstract. Insight, inspiration, and hypotheses guide an intuitive individual's perception. The intuitive looks at possibilities and generalizes. Intuitive individuals are flexible and interested in ideas and alternatives.

Think about yourself. What about you? Are you more sensing or more intuitive?

How do you judge the world. The decision-making functions are thinking and feeling. The thinking individual is objective and uses facts, evidence, and logic. Thinkers are well organized and establish procedures but are not comfortable expressing their feelings. Conversely, feeling individuals view the world in a personalized fashion. Their emotions influence decisions; they are subjective and spontaneous. Harmony and approval are important to them.

Have you decided? Are you more thinking or more feeling?

Let's look at the permutations. There are four possible combinations. An individual can be a sensing-thinker or sensing-feeler, an intuitive-thinker or an intuitive-feeler. This can all seem quite confusing if you are still trying to integrate multiple intelligences into your thinking, but it will all come together. An individual's style preference is the combination of perception and judgment functions. Here are the possibilities:

Sensing-Thinking: Practical, disciplined, orderly. Sensing-thinking teachers use lecture, demonstration, drill, and competitive games. Sensing-thinking students are most comfortable with structure and facts–recalling, sequencing, categorizing, competing, and collaborating. It's important to them to receive feedback which lets them know if they are right or wrong.

Sensing-Feeling: Cooperative, empathetic, personal. Sensing-feeling teachers use collaborative learning, hold class discussions, and work with small groups. The sensing-feeling student enjoys going slowly, being physical, and is comfortable being

81

GA1494

part of a team, empathizing, and personalizing. Affective experiences which include preferring and valuing connect these students to school; being valued and feeling important is essential to them.

Intuitive-Thinking: Analytic, logical, ingenious. Intuitive-thinking teachers enjoy intellectual challenge; look at issues globally; focus on ideas; and use debate, discussion, and lecture. The intuitive-thinking student enjoys questioning, comparing and contrasting; problem-solving; determining cause and effect; predicting; detecting patterns; and summarizing or explaining. Intuitive thinkers appreciate a thoughtful critique of their work.

Intuitive-Feeling: Innovative, insightful, enthusiastic. Intuitive-feeling teachers incorporate divergent thinking, creative expression, and alternatives, and are adept at combining old ideas with new ones. Intuitive-feeling students enjoy imagining, exploring possibilities, setting their own goals, and producing original work. Your reaction and appreciation are sought by the intuitive-feeling student.

Take a careful look at the information above; think about your favorite lessons and how (and to whom) you taught them.

Think about which children excelled and which children got left behind.

Think about courses you might have taken had your teachers known a little more about how you learned best.

Consider how your style influences your teaching.

Consider how the varying styles of your students influence their learning.

Recognize that each student in your class has a dominant style as well as a style which is uncomfortable.

Know that the teaching strategy which you choose for a particular lesson will influence the type of thinking you will elicit from your students.

At this point, you are well aware that learning about style and learning about multiple intelligences is learning about differences. It is also about teaching to those differences. It is about adding to your "bag of tricks." A teacher's repertoire of teaching strategies is in direct proportion to success in the classroom. Strategies which address individual student needs or curricular needs cannot help but influence your teaching. As you reflect on style and multiple intelligences, remember that the information here is cursory; it barely scratches the surface. Consider these as beginner's lessons and refer to the work of Howard Gardner, Isabel Myers, Richard Strong, Harvey Silver, Robert Hanson, Rita Dunn, Anthony Gregorc, Bruce Joyce, and, of course, Carl Jung on whose work theirs is based.

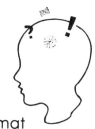

Lesson Sample Menus

The next few pages offer some actual lesson samples using a planning format much like a menu. This works well when designing questions and assignments that integrate what is known about the varying styles. Refer back to pages 81 and 82 for the characteristics and preferences of the styles. Some thoughts on how to structure or phrase tasks for your students are below.

Sensing-Thinking	Intuitive-Thinking	Sensing-Feeling	Intuitive-Feeling
Write definitions, write an article, find examples, follow directions, fill in blanks, keep records, record facts, list, recall, sequence, make something useful, make a display, think about, demonstrate, dramatize	Write an essay, compare and contrast, ask questions, prove, summarize, cause and effect, analyze, evaluate, argue for or against, explain, look for similarities and differences, research, use information to show, design an experiment, plan, forecast consequences, organize, direct, debate	Relate a personal experience, describe your feelings, which do you prefer, choose one and tell why, which is more important, what are some advantages and disadvantages, if you were. . . what would you do? role play, keep a journal, write a poem, give an oral report, work with a friend	Create a story, generate some ideas, find a pattern, look for solutions, dramatize a scene, choose lines from a story and illustrate, design or diagram, use imagination, what do you think happened next, how would you solve, discuss, what would you do

Many teachers enjoy teaching their students about learning styles. This allows students to reflect upon their learning and classroom assignments and then evolve into metacognitive exercises, bringing an awareness of the thinking processes. If you involve students in this process, it would make sense for you to designate the style when making the assignment. However, the questions may simply be written on the board so students can choose the ones they prefer. To encourage students to stretch themselves, assign work in two styles.

GA1494

Quotations in Search of Authors

No Limits but the Sky by Susanna Palomares is a book of motivational quotations chosen because they cause us to think about how one's thoughts can influence one's actions. Most of the quotations in the book have known authors, but the originators of the words of wisdom on this page are unknown.

Read through the quotations below and choose one of the four activities listed on the chart.

"Of all the things you wear, your expression is the most important."

"It's a rare person who doesn't get discouraged. Whether it happens to us or to someone we know, the answer to this dilemma centers around one word: perseverance."

"Life is partly what you make it, and partly how you take it."

"A friend is a push when you've stopped, a word when you're lonely, a guide when you're searching, a smile when you're sad, a song when you're glad."

Sensing-Thinking	Intuitive-Thinking	Sensing-Feeling	Intuitive-Feeling
Choose the quotation that you think gives the best advice. Copy it on a large sheet of construction paper. Find a book whose theme repeats the quotation's message.	Choose the quotation that you think gives the best advice. Write a paragraph explaining why it is useful. Name a well-known individual who could have said it, and make up two or three questions you would ask that person about it.	Select the quotation you like best. Write a description of an event in your life when the quotation would have applied. Who do you know that you think could have said this? When would that person have said it?	Select a quotation which you believe to be the most valuable. Explain why you chose it. What famous person do you think could have said this? Why would he or she have said it?

GA1494

Chester's Way

In *Chester's Way*, author Kevin Henkes writes about a friendship between two mice. Read the book, and then complete one of the four activites listed on the chart.

Sensing-Thinking	Intuitive-Thinking	Sensing-Feeling	Intuitive-Feeling
List ten examples of the special ways Chester and Wilson had of doing things.	What caused Chester and Wilson to accept Lily as a friend? What did they learn from her?	Have you ever had an experience like this? Tell what happened.	What would you do if you were Victor? Write about it. What do you think the author would have written?

_____

_____

_____

_____

_____

_____

_____

_____

_____

_____

_____

_____

GA1494

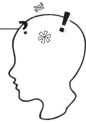

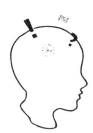

What Can You Learn from Television?

In your cooperative groups decide on a television program which you will all watch. Be sure to get permission from your family. Then answer all of the questions below. You may choose within your group who is to answer which question, and you may help one another with the answers. You are all responsible for completing the information at the top of the sheet and for presenting your group's findings to the rest of the class.

Name _____

Program _____

Why did you choose it? _____

_____

Sensing-Thinking	Who was the star of this program? What character did he or she play? Give a physical description of that character. Tell in five sentences what happened on the show.
Intuitive-Thinking	Did the characters in the program you watched act like real people would act? What was realistic? What was unrealistic? Who was the least realistic character? Why?
Sensing-Feeling	Describe how you felt watching this program. Would you allow your own children to watch this program? Why or why not? Would you watch this program again? Why or why not?
Intuitive-Feeling	What do you think a viewer would learn watching this program? What other program is this one most like? In what ways is it different?

In your group, decide on a way to present your answers to the rest of the class.

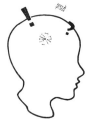

GA1494

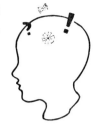

Presidents of the Twentieth Century

Complete four assignments for this unit. Choose from either chart below. Be sure to choose one from each learning style.

Name _____

Please circle the numbers of the questions you answered and attach your answers to this sheet.

Sensing-Thinking	1. Make a time line showing the Presidents of the United States who have held office during this time period.
Intuitive-Thinking	2. Compare and contrast the terms of two of the Presidents who have held office during this time.
Sensing-Feeling	3. Which of the Presidents do you feel did the best job? Write a letter to him telling him why you think he was a good President.
Intuitive-Feeling	4. Design a museum exhibit for the President you most admire. Include items which refer to events that occurred during that President's term in office.

Sensing-Thinking	5. What are the ten most important facts you learned about the President you most admire?
Intuitive-Thinking	6. Write one question you would ask of each of the Presidents who has held office during this time.
Sensing-Feeling	7. Think of an important event that occurred during one of the presidencies and write an imaginary diary entry from that President's point of view.
Intuitive-Feeling	8. If you had been one of the Presidents, what would you have done differently?

Brainwaves

Stress affects all of us and stress in the classroom affects learning. Picture this scene from your childhood: "Today, students, we're going to have a pop quiz." Did it strike fear into your heart? Did the hairs stand up on the back of your neck? Did you do poorly on the quiz? Renate and Geoffrey Caine report in *Making Connections: Teaching and the Human Brain* that learning involves our entire physiology, that threat and challenge, as well as boredom affect our learning and our performance. Learning is diminished when there is threat or stress, facilitated when there is challenge.[1]

How many of your students come to school ready to learn? Many who come into our classrooms from dysfunctional homes are frequently so stressed that they cannot learn. Your classroom may be the only island of safety in their lives.

Is there a best stress? Researchers report that high stress releases adrenaline and blocks thinking, and very low levels of stress don't create sufficient neural connections. The answer, they say, is low to medium stress. A little anxiety improves learning through increasing sensitivity. (The question is how to figure out when you've achieved that.) A relaxed and focused environment is purported to reduce performance anxiety. Cooperative learning strategies such as Teams as Teachers or Testwise are designed to be low stress and make learning interesting and fun. Brain-compatible research supports the notion that learning should not be a goal in and of itself but a by-product of a "play" situation and it therefore reinforces the use of cooperative strategies.

The National Institute for Mental Health went one step further in researching this area. They discovered that neuron activity was greater on harder tasks and, while performance might be lower, the brain was more activated. What does this mean for classroom instruction? Don't mix easy and hard tasks–stepladder tasks so that each is more complex than the one before. Increasing levels of challenge creates more interest.

---

1.   Quoted with permission.

GA1494

The brain is constantly searching for meaning. It does this in a number of ways, one of them being patterning. According to the Caines, patterning creates personal meaning. Visual-spatial learners should have visuals in the classroom which help them to construct meaning. Information which can be mapped, charted, or pictured should be in the learning environment to encourage other learners to also build their skills in this area. When the brain finds relevance, patterning also occurs. This reiterates the significance of whole language and thematic teaching because they provide a basis for extracting meaning.

In much the same realm, the brain's response to sensory stimuli complements more focused stimuli. In classrooms where the bulletin boards haven't been changed in years, the students in those rooms have been missing something. Something so mundane as bulletin boards actually can influence learning. Every visual signal is given meaning by the brain and should be organized to enhance learning. While they may not be under constant scrutiny, apparently bulletin boards, background music (for some students), and exposure to art are important as a means of enhancing learning–even if they are peripheral.

For patterning to work, the emotions must be involved. Feelings and attitudes and mindsets and social interactions must be taken into consideration. A supportive environment and effective communication are integral for patterning and thus for meaning. Cooperative classrooms which engage students and require emotional arousal facilitate patterning. The signals (or stimuli) which teachers give, even if they're peripheral, work actively to engage students. The enthusiasm you show sends a message to your students–"This is worthwhile and important for you to know." Students can be very discerning about both the messages we consciously send and those we unconsciously transmit.

GA1494

The left and right hemispheres of the brain have different functions and organize information in different ways, but the hemispheres working together put everything into context.

People can be more right-brain oriented than left-brained oriented. The following characteristics should be considered when assessing student needs related to classroom instruction.

Left (Analytic)	Right (Global)
Verbal	Visual, Tactile, Kinesthetic
Responds to Word Meanings	Responds to Word Feelings
Recalls Facts, Dates	Recalls Images, Patterns
Sequential	Random
Processes Information in Linear Fashion	Processes Information in Chunks
Responds to Logical Appeal	Responds to Emotional Appeal
Trusts Logic	Trusts Intuition
Looks Organized	Looks Disorganized
Plans Ahead	Spontaneous
Punctual	Less Punctual
Reflective	Impulsive
Recalls Names	Recalls Faces
Rarely Gestures When Speaking	Frequently Gestures When Speaking

Additional research in this area suggests that the brain needs change, that hemispheric dominance changes from left to right every one to two hours. In the classroom this means adapting or planning activities which alternate from linear to holistic, from skills to concepts, from parts to wholes. This is therefore another argument in favor of thematic and whole language teaching.

GA1494

In research done in Russia, this information was reinforced from a different perspective. Dr. Victor Shatalov discovered that students learned better when the teacher instruction alternated between presenting information in condensed form and presenting it in detailed form. Students were to recall information in condensed format and then were tested in detailed format. This supports the idea of change—for presenting a global overview initially, followed by detailed information, and then a global summary.

We learn consciously and unconsciously at the same time. Students must process not only what they have learned, but how they learned it. Students who process their experiences remember them. The active processing techniques involved in reflection and metacognition put students in charge of their learning. This may involve teaching students about their own learning styles. It most certainly involves orchestrating situations so students have experiences on which to reflect.

We have two kinds of memory systems. Rote memory, which identifies facts and skills in isolation, is organized differently in the brain and needs practice because it is generally unrelated to understanding. Spatial memory records our experiences and helps us find meaning. It is meaningfulness which is essential. An experimental focus provides a memory base which cannot help but give students greater capability because it enables them to always be working in context. Thematic, integrated teaching lends itself to all that brain-based research supports, specifically teaching for meaning. Cooperative strategies are built for meaning and fit into thematic teaching as if they were intended solely for that purpose. The information on style and intelligences should fit nicely into your spatial memory because there is a context for it—the children you are teaching.

GA1494

Bibliography

Aliki, *We Are Best Friends*, New York: William Morrow & Company, Inc., 1982.

Blos, Joan W., *Old Henry*, New York: Morrow Jr. Books, 1987.

Blume, Judy, *The One in the Middle Is the Green Kangaroo*, New York: Dell Publishing Co., 1982.

Bohdal, Susi, *The Magic Honey Jar*, publishing information not available.

Caine, Renate Nummela and Geoffrey Caine, *Making Connections: Teaching and the Human Brain*, Alexandria, Virginia: Association for Supervision and Curriculum Development, 1991. (Quoted with permission)

Cooney, Barbara, *Miss Rumphius*, New York: Puffin Books, 1985.

Gilson, Jamie, *Hello, My Name Is Scrambled Eggs*, New York: Minstrel Books, 1991.

Henkes, Kevin, *Chester's Way*, New York: Puffin Books, 1989.

McCloskey, Robert, *Lentil*, New York: Puffin Books, 1978.

McGraw, Eloise, *The Seventeenth Swap*, Mahweh, New Jersey: Troll Associates, 1987.

Manes, Stephen, *Be a Perfect Person in Just Three Days,* New York: Bantam Books Inc., 1987.

Miles, Miska, *Annie and the Old One*, Boston: Little Brown and Company, 1971.

Moeri, Louise, *Save Queen of Sheba*, New York: Avon Books, 1981.

Nixon, Joan Lowery, *The Gift*, New York: Macmillan Children's Group, 1983.

Palomares, Susanna, *No Limits but the Sky*, Spring Valley, California: Innerchoice Publishing, 1992.

Renzulli, Joseph S. and Sally M., Reis, *The Schoolwide Enrichment Model: A Comprehensive Plan for Educational Excellence*, Connecticut: Creative Learning Press, 1985.

Rylant, Cynthia, *When I Was Young in the Mountains*, New York: Dutton Childrens Books, 1985.

Schlissel, Lillian, *Women's Diaries of the Westward Journey*, New York: Schachen Books, 1982.

Shreve, Susan, *Lily and the Runaway Baby*, New York: Random Books for Young Readers, 1987.

Silver, Harvey F. and J. Robert Hanson, *The TLC Learning Style Inventory,*, Moorestown, New Jersey: Hanson Silver Strong & Associates.

Smith, Robert Kimmel, *The War With Grandpa*, New York: Dell Yearling, 1984.

Steig, William, *Abel's Island*, Toronto: McGraw Hill Ryerson Ltd., 1977.

Strong, Richard, et al, "New Strategies, New Visions," *Educational Leadership*, October 1986.

Viorst, Judith, *Alexander and the Terrible, Horrible, No Good, Very Bad Day*, New York: Macmillan Children's Group, 1989.

GA1494